I0707079

Dark Psychology

Learn the Secrets of Emotional Influence With the Techniques Against NLP, Deception, Brainwashing, and Mind Control to Obtain What You Want and Stop Being Manipulated

By Travis Harper

Table of Contents

Introduction

Congratulations for downloading your copy of *"Dark Psychology: Learn the Secrets of Emotional Influence With the Techniques Against NLP, Deception, Brainwashing, and Mind Control to Obtain What You Want and Stop Being Manipulated"* and thank you for doing so. The following chapters will discuss in-depth on dark psychology and get the knowledge of how to manipulate people to propel your life forward.

In chapter one, I'll introduce dark psychology. Further, my book discusses on persuasion. You will learn about the elements of persuasion and the ways that you will use persuasion to succeed in leadership. On the other hand, the book is clear on what to do when there is resistance in persuasion. Read through to learn more.

In chapter two, the book begins a discussion on Neuro-Linguistic Programming (NLP). Here, you will get the knowledge of NLP, how it is used and in what circumstances. You will further find the NLP techniques, a guide to using NLP and also how NLP is used in the manipulation of the mind.

In chapter three, it is all about the psychology of manipulation. How do you take charge and control negative manipulation in your life? You will get all these answers as well as the knowledge of how to take note of manipulators.

In chapter four, the discussion is all about mind controls. Now, this is what manipulators do to your mind to drive you into taking action. This includes brainwashing, coercion, hypnosis and much more that you will learn.

In chapter five, you will find a discussion on the use of your mind to succeed. Here, you will learn how to attract positive people in your life. You will further know about influencing people at work as well as gaining the necessary skills that will enhance your leadership. Read through and find out much more.

Finally, chapter six is a discussion on the manipulation theories. Here, you will get the knowledge of why things happen as they do, for example, why do you feel the urge to give back in kind when someone helps you. All these are theories and principles discussed in this chapter.

There are plenty of books on this subject on the market, so thanks again for choosing this one! Every effort was made to ensure it is full of as much useful information as possible, please enjoy it!

Chapter 1: Introduction to Dark Psychology

What Dark Psychology is

Dark Psychology is deception and mind manipulation science and art. Although Psychology is the reality of human behavior and is fundamental to our emotions, behaviors, and experiences, the term Dark Psychology is the process through which individuals use motivation, persuasion, deception, and intimidation techniques to get whatever they want. You may have gone through this in different aspects.

Dark Psychology Triad

Let us briefly go through the dark psychology triad that will help you identify the negative characteristics of negative manipulators.

- **Narcissism** - This involves selfishness, superiority, and lack of compassion.
- **Machiavellianism** - Such humans often use deception to manipulate or take advantage of people and do not have any sense of ethics.
- **Psychopathic** - Although often attractive and polite, it is marked by impulsiveness, greed, lack of compassion and guilt.

Nobody seems to want to be a deceptive target, but more often than not this occurs. We might not be subject to someone particular to the Dark Triad, but regularly, we face dark psychology tactics with normal, ordinary people like you and me.

Through advertisements, web advertising, sales techniques, and even the actions of our boss, these methods are often identified. If you already have children (particularly adolescents) you will more than undoubtedly encounter these tactics as your children experience habits to get whatever they want and pursue autonomy. People you can trust and adore often use covert manipulation and dark persuasion. Here are some of the techniques used most often by ordinary people on a daily basis.

- **Love Flooding** - This entails compliments, intimacy or trying to butter someone to make a request
- **Lying** - This has exaggeration, falsehoods, half-truths, untrue
- **Love Denial Tales** - This involves the removal of love and attention avoiding the individual or silent treatment

The motivation behind this article isn't to disclose to you how to abstain from being controlled and misused. Or maybe, it's to help all of us to remember that it is so natural to fall into utilizing these strategies to get what we need. I need to move you to evaluate your strategies in all everyday issues, including your work, initiative, sentimental connections, child-rearing, and companionships.

While some people who use dim strategies know exactly what they are doing and are purposeful in manipulating you to get what they need, others are using dull and irritating strategies without being fully aware of it. A good number of these people took their folks into the approaches during the youth. Others have mistakenly taken the techniques in their high school years and adulthood. They mistakenly used a control strategy, and it succeeded. They've got what they need. In this way, we tend to use tactics to help them get their way.

Sometimes, individuals are prepared to utilize these strategies. Preparing programs that show dull, deceptive mental and influence strategies are normally deals or showcasing programs. A large number of these projects use dull strategies to make a brand or sell an item with the sole reason for serving themselves or their organization, not the client. A large number of these preparation projects persuade individuals that utilizing such strategies is alright and is to support the purchaser. Since their lives will be vastly improved when they buy the item or administration.

The intention is what distinguishes the terms persuasion and dark persuasion. A persuader may try to convince people to do things without thinking about particular strategies or inspiration and without any kind of true understanding of the individual they are trying to convince. A persuader may be worried about developing the most good for the majority of people, like a diplomat who wants to prevent conflict between two global powers by developing political connections where none is existing. A persuader could grab desperately at straws trying to hold to something. A dark persuader sees the larger picture at all times. He knows who he is attempting to convince, what encourages them, and to achieve, he strategically knows how far he needs to take the technique. He's usually unconcerned about his manipulation's ethics. He may see "doing all the proper thing" as an advantage, but it does not have to be his greatest justification. The activities of a dark persuader do not always come down into the intersecting area in the Venn diagram of morality and ego-gratification. A dark persuader will see what he or she wants and will come up with a way of obtaining it by any method.

Persuasion

Persuasion is the art of convincing people to commit to what you are telling or selling to them. It needs you to tune their mind, from a place of aggressiveness to a point of acceptance.

Elements of Persuasion

Persuasion is a piece of communication procedure. The five essential components of persuasion include the source of information, the message being communicated, medium the message passes through, and also public and effect. How about we take a gander at every component quickly.

The nature of the source; the individual or association from where the original message comes from is significant in affecting how successful the message is. The source must have believability. The more dependable the source, the more convincing it is. The most ideal approach to stay trustworthy is to be straightforward and exact constantly. Being preferred by your group of spectators is critical to have the option to convince them.

The message is the solitary perspective over which an essayist has absolute control. You choose what to state and when and how to state it. The best influential written information utilizes both accurate and passionate contentions.

Even though the medium of message transmission is like the message itself might be fairly misrepresented, it speaks to the fact that it is so imperative to utilize the correct channel to contact your group of the target audience. Spoken correspondence is bound to realize productivity, some state, yet the composed word accomplishes better understanding. On the off chance that you keep your message brief, your intended interest group will concentrate on your message, not another person's translation.

You should know your crowd. The choices about what to state and where to put that message to arrive at your objective will be educated by your insight into that target. Keep in mind, your target audience will, in general, overlook things, regardless of how solid and explicit the message is, so you may need to rehash your key focuses. As in everything business, there is a main concern or impact: Did the group of audience do what you needed them to do? As we approach the election period, and watch, tune in to and read all the data from applicants, those pursuing positions will discover rapidly whether their messages convinced us to decide in favor of them.

However, in business, it might take much more time to tell whether a message had its expected impact. Promoting attempts to bring issues to light. PR endeavors to convince. What's more, some of the time, the impacts of those procedures are not understood for a generous measure of time. Understanding the components of the enticing procedure may assist you with improving your business interchanges, better arrive at your intended interest group and improve your main concern.

Emotional Persuasion for Success in Leadership

All that a leader does in communication is persuasion. That is the thing that pioneers do. They convince individuals to cooperate, to accomplish more than they at any point figured they couldn't, to go after obviously unthinkable objectives, to set individual interests aside in any event briefly for some bigger gathering reason. Persuasion means altering somebody's perspective. You should note that, if the mind isn't changed, the individual hasn't been convinced. It's that basic. So, a pioneer's responsibility is to change minds, to push adherents to settle on new choices.

The making of decisions is in a general a sense of emotional state. Ongoing cerebrum research shows that if you weaken the piece of the mind that is concerned about feelings, through a stroke or other mind injury, individuals can't decide. That is because, apart from obfuscating our capacity to choose, feelings make it conceivable. It works along these lines: We label our encounters and the memories we have with feelings to have the option to recover them at vital minutes after the fact on. For instance, if we get our hand burnt on a hot stove, we label our memory of the occurrence with a feeling. That feeling makes the memory simple to recover sometime in the not too distant future, and we always remember not to contact the following hot stove. No feeling, no recovery. No recovery, no choice.

Since influence lies unequivocally at the focal point of great leadership, of changing your mind and deciding, an emotional procedure is a key to what effective leaders do. More than that, it's a procedure that needs both scholarly artfulness and the nonverbal aptitude. An effective leader, at the end of the day, must be okay with arguments that take an emotional state and agreeable in their skin making and reacting to those contentions. Mindfulness is basic; understanding your very own enthusiastic propensities and reactions is basic in case you will bring out and shape passionate reactions in others.

At last, basic leadership is nine-tenths feeling and one-tenth scholarly support. Most thinking about basic leadership is ex post facto support of choices previously made on enthusiastic grounds. We choose to go for a stretch second-quarter objective, for instance, since we need it, or it feels right, or some other similarly impalpable explanation. At that point, we gather scholarly explanations behind the choice that we've just made, to legitimize it to ourselves.

How about we go above and beyond. The vast majority of us have a practical comprehension of how our brains work that goes something like this: My very conscious mind is in control. I get musings, similar to, I need to walk over that side and converse with that individual, and afterward I direct my body to follow up on those considerations. It's as though a little executive was sitting in my mind getting out requests and managing everything.

Once more, ongoing mind research turns that conventional thought on its head. The vast majority of our intellectual competence is oblivious. The proportion of neurons that administer unconscious ideas to a conscious idea is about 10 million to one. We are fundamentally unconscious creatures on a programmed pilot. To be sure, it must be that way. That unconscious mind keeps us alive. If we needed to ponder everything from keeping our heart siphoning to breathing to dodging enormous savage warm-blooded animals, we'd be dead in a matter of seconds.

That is how we advanced, however now that we're in a cutting-edge world, a portion of those oblivious perspectives trips us up. For instance, when we see a huge gathering of individuals - actually, well before we're deliberately mindful of them- - our unconscious cerebrum gets down to business preparing us for battle or flight. What's more, since we have neurons in our minds that get on the feelings of everybody around us, when one individual in a gathering goes into battle or flight, the entire gathering before long does.

Back to authority correspondence. When you as a leader remain before a crowd of your staff attempting to convince them to go for that second-quarter goal achievement, even before you start speaking, you notice that everybody in the group has started to

8

freeze, at any rate, due to the battle or flight signals you convey without being deliberately mindful of them.

All of a sudden, the activity of influence is more complicated than you may have anticipated. How would you convince a room brimming with worried individuals to work more enthusiastically or switch drastically or surrender get-away and ends of the week to spare the organization? You do it by taking that group of staff on a passionate basic leadership process, starting with a genuine affirmation of the position they are at this moment.

In any case, before you address that group of your employees, you have to do some prior assignment as a pioneer to deal with your very own oblivious non-verbal communication, so you can convey messages of transparency and association instead of peril and separation. If you don't begin with that, your time of service as a leader will be over before it has started.

Authority is an influence. Influence is enthusiastic. The feeling is oblivious. Pioneers need to ace their unconscious enthusiastic perspectives to succeed. It's basic work for any individual who needs to convince others to accomplish anything beneficial.

Ways to Overcome Persuasion Resistance

You may work hard in convincing a group of people but still realize that they are not being receptive. It can feel depressing because it is a joy to be of impact and to see that our work bears fruit. Therefore, worry not because I got you. Here are the top ways the brain withstands persuasion and how they can be broken down or sustained by both.

- Therapeutic vaccinations work by giving you a tad bit of the illness with the goal that your body can become acclimated to it and battle off a full assault later on. Mental vaccinations against influence work in a similar way. At the point when individuals have been set up with counter-contentions, they think that it is simpler to the battle of influence endeavors.

When Convincing: What counter-contention will individuals know? Maintain a strategic distance from the 'standard thing' contentions in your influence endeavor. Rather, utilize another edge they haven't pondered previously.

When in Persuasion Resistance: Open yourself to various kinds of contentions and counter-contentions you will probably confront. At the point when you recognize what's coming, it's simpler to protect yourself mentally. Search for circuitous influence endeavors: maybe it's a similar old contention made in a marginally extraordinary manner.

- At the point when we can see the influence endeavor coming, it's a lot simpler to marshal our safeguards. Obtrusive promoting, party political communication and the rest: our guards are up so it's harder to overcome.

When Convincing: Don't flag your endeavor ahead of time. Attempt to redirect consideration from the influence endeavor by concealing it inside a harmless message. Underline how you are 'simply talking' or 'just examining' something.

When Opposing Influence: Attempt to spot influence endeavors that are enveloped with social weight or as a diversion. For instance: Discover increasingly about the mystery love of the entertainer!

- Individuals don't care for being determined what to do or having their opportunity confined. It can even prompt a boomerang impact where advising individuals not to accomplish something prompts them to need to do it more.

  When Persuading, it is necessary to try and avoid limiting individuals' free self; rather make them feel they have choices and space and this can work in your favor of the potential benefit

On the other hand, when opposing persuasion: consider whether the influence endeavor is limiting your opportunity. If it is, at that point would it be a good idea for you to oblige it? Then again, is the individual underscoring how free you are to convince you?

- In the wake of being convinced, individuals regularly play out a kind of rude awakening. Have I consented to something I didn't intend to? Would I have concurred on the off chance that I knew, at that point what I know now? If not, at that point drop the entire thing!

When convincing them don't give individuals the ideal opportunity for a rude awakening. Under time weight individuals think that it's hard to think.
When opposing persuasion take a break a short time later to consider whether you would at present consent to it. Watch out for time weight or restricted arrangements these are intended to alternate route levelheaded procedures and make us bounce directly in.

- It's the most common guard of all: considering why they are not right and you are correct. While in persuasion, firmly held convictions are hard to assault. Have a go at being slippery and avoiding them. Limit your point to make it less undermining or cause the relationship to appear to be increasingly cooperative

  When opposing persuasion consider who else concurs with you. This reinforces your situation by utilizing social affirmation. Be careful about disguised endeavors to convince.

- At the point when individuals effectively safeguard themselves against an endeavor at influence, their unique position gets more grounded. Let's assume

I'm attempting to convince you to color your hair blue and you think you'll look crazy. Except if I set forward a superior case than, saying it will be crazy, you'll be significantly more against it a while later.

When persuading makes your first endeavor to convince a solid one, don't go in irresolute or you could simply build opposition over the long haul.

When Opposing Influence: On the off chance that you realize the influence endeavor is coming and you have counter-contentions prepared then your opposition will just make you more grounded.

- Most often persuasion endeavors to regularly utilize the contention from power, sort of like: I am your parent so I know what is better for you. But like any youngster, we need to revolt so we assault authority.

  When you are persuading ensure your certifications are unshakable. If they're not, discover somebody whose authority is unchallenged. Individuals normally concede to the individuals who have (or seem to have) authority.

When Opposing Influence: Assault the wellspring of the message. Use negative feelings like outrage or aggravation and ascribe them to the supposed power figure. Be amazingly suspicious of any individual who depends simply on power to impact.

- **Being Sharp and Focused**
  The resistance is almost effortless when we feel alert and focused. That is the point at which you are better ready to raise counter-contentions, support your position, take note of influence endeavors coming, etc.

  When in persuasion and notice that individuals are worn out, their resistances are usually down. If they could be alert, would they be able to be worn out or their obstruction blunted by a frontal assault? What's more, would you be able to decrease their inspiration to present resistance?

When Opposing Persuasion: Be careful of tiredness. Never go out to shop when you're extremely in hunger, purchase a vehicle when you're in desperation or converse with a sales rep when you're half-occupied. Perceive times when you're probably going to be feeble and storage room yourself until the vitality levels are renewed.

- **Lack of Listening**

  Often, the most straightforward methods for opposing resistance are the least difficult. You leave, turn off the TV or shut out the automaton of other individuals' perspectives by murmuring the subject to the team.

  While persuasion does you have their complete focus? If by any chance they are not, at that point it's difficult to be successful. When they are centered around you, start with the most intriguing piece of the contention to attract their attention towards you.

  When opposing persuasion would you say you are truly overlooking it? We are more effectively influenced than we might suspect. The most conjecture that it's other individuals who are affected by adverts or political messages, not ourselves. Don't simply turn it down, but also put it off.

Chapter 2: NLP-Neuro Linguistic Programming

NLP stands for Neuro-Linguistic Programming. Neuro is the mind, Linguistic is the language and programming refers to the functionality of the Neuro language. Defined, NLP is the study of your mind. In NLP, it is a belief that each one of us has enough resources to make a positive impact on our own life. We should make this less difficult with a model.

Have you at any point attempted to speak with somebody who didn't communicate in your language, and they couldn't get you? The great case of this is the point at which somebody goes out to a café in a Foreign nation and they think they requested some beef, however, when the nourishment appears, it turns out they requested chicken.

This is the sort of relationship that the vast majority of us have with our very own unconscious mind. We may think we are requesting up some more cash, an upbeat, sound relationship, harmony with our relatives, and having the option to adhere to a solid eating routine... however except if that is the thing that appearing, at that point something is most likely becoming mixed up in interpretation.

There is a saying in NLP that the conscious mind is responsible for goal setting, and the unconscious mind is the goal-getter. Your conscious personality isn't out to get you–rather, it's out TO GET FOR YOU anything you desire throughout everyday life. Nonetheless, if you don't have the foggiest idea of how to convey what you need appropriately, it will continue bringing steaming bowls of liver stew out of the kitchen.

Indeed, proceed at present and consider, if there would one thing you could transform, one habit you could cut, what might it be?

- Maybe it is to try to avoid panicking during work introductions?

- Stop lingering and investing such a great amount of energy on Face book?
- Not eat up an entire pack of potato chips or tub of frozen yogurt at once?

Whatever it is, understand that your conscious mind just only does that since it feels that is the thing that you need. 'Hello, here is your procrastination alongside a side of tension. I've likewise advised the valet to raise your psychological weight according to your solicitation. Will you need anything else?

Neuro-Linguistic Programming resembles a client's manual for the brain, and taking training in NLP resembles figuring out how to get familiar with the language of your brain so that the supportive "server" that is your unconscious will, at last, comprehend what you deeply desire. NLP is simply the investigation of astounding correspondence both with yourself and with others. It was created by demonstrating amazing communicators and specialists who got results with their customers. NLP is a lot of apparatuses and systems, yet it is far beyond that. It is a disposition and an approach of realizing how to accomplish your objectives and get results.

Techniques of NLP

Now let us go through the NLP techniques that will help you improve your life is a positive manner.

Separation

Have you at any point been in a circumstance that gave you an awful feeling? Possibly you have encountered something that gets you down each time you experience it. Maybe, on the other hand, you get apprehensive in certain work circumstances where you need to talk freely. Perhaps you get timid when you need to move toward that "unique somebody" you are eyeing. While these sentiments of trouble, apprehension or timidity appear to be programmed or relentless, NLP methods of separation can be of immense assistance. Here is what you could do;

- Recognize the feeling, for example, dread, rage, distress, aversion of a circumstance) that you need to dispose of yourself.
- Envision that you can buy out of your body and glance back at yourself, experiencing the whole situation from an onlooker's point of view
- Notice that the inclination changes drastically

For an additional lift, envision that you can move out of your body taking a gander at yourself, at that point, glide out of this body once more, so you're seeing yourself, taking a look at yourself. This twofold separation should take the negative feeling off practically any minor circumstance

Reframing of Content

Attempt this method when you feel that a circumstance is negative or defenseless. Reframing will take any negative circumstance and enable you by changing the significance of the experience into something positive.

For instance, suppose that your relationship closes. That may appear to be horrendous superficially, however, how about we reframe it. What are the potential advantages of being single? For instance, you're presently open to other potential connections. You likewise have the opportunity to do what you need, when you need it. What's more, you've taken in significant learning from this relationship that will enable you to have greater relationships later on. These are for the most part instances of reframing a circumstance that you have gone through. By reframing the importance of the separation, you give yourself an alternate encounter of it.

In anticipated circumstances, it's normal to frenzy or spotlight on dread, however, this equitable prompt more issues. Conversely, moving your concentration in the manner in which simply portrayed encourages you to clear your head and make capable, impartial choices.

Anchor Yourself

Anchoring yourself encourages you to relate any ideal positive passionate reaction with a specific expression or sensation. At the point when you pick a positive feeling or thought and purposely interface it to a basic signal, you can trigger this anchor whenever you're feeling low, and your emotions will promptly change.

It is important to distinguish what you need to feel, it could be a certainty, bliss, smoothness, and so on.
Choose where you might want to put this anchor on your body, for example, you could pull your ear cartilage, contact your knuckle or crushing a fingernail. This physical touch will enable you to trigger the positive inclination voluntarily. It doesn't make a difference where you pick, as long as it is a one of a kind touches that you don't contact for whatever else.
Think about a period in the past when you felt that state (e.g., certainty). Rationally return to that time and get in your body, glancing through your very own eyes and remembering that time. Change your non-verbal communication to coordinate the memory and the state. See what you saw, hear what you heard and feel the inclination as you recollect that memory. You will start to feel that state. This is like recounting to a companion an amusing story from an earlier time, and as you "get into" the story, you begin to snicker once more, since you "partner" to the story and "remember" it.

As you return to the memory, contact, pull, or press the region on your body that you picked. You will feel the inclination swell while you remember the memory. Discharge the touch the minute the passionate state pinnacles and starts to wear off. This will make a neurological boost reaction that will trigger the state at whatever point you make that touch once more. To feel that state (e.g., Confidence), simply contact yourself a similar way once more. To make the reaction significantly more grounded, think about another memory where you felt that state, return and remember it through your very own eyes, and grapple the state on a similar spot as in the past. Each time you include another memory, the grapple turns out to be increasingly powerful and will trigger a more grounded reaction

Building a Great Connection

This is a simple arrangement of NLP methods, yet they can assist you with coexisting with for all intents and purposes anybody. There are bunches of approaches to construct affinity with someone else. One of the snappiest and viable ways originates from NLP. This system includes inconspicuously reflecting someone else's non-verbal communication, manner of speaking, and words. Individuals like individuals who are such as themselves. By unobtrusively reflecting the other individual, the mind shoots "reflect neurons," delight sensors in the cerebrum, which understand enjoying for anybody reflecting them.

The procedure is basic: Stand or sit how the other individual is sitting. Tilt your head a similar way. Grin when they grin. Mirror their outward appearance. Fold your legs when they cross theirs. Mirror their voice, and so on. The way of making oblivious compatibility is nuance. If you are excessively clear, the other individual may see intentionally, which would in all likelihood break affinity. So, keep your reflecting normal and quiet.

Persuasion and Influence

While a great part of crafted by NLP is devoted to helping individuals take out negative feelings, restricting convictions, unfortunate propensities, struggle, and that's only the tip of the iceberg, another piece of NLP is committed to how to morally impact and convince others. One of the coaches in the field was a man called Milton H. Erickson. He was a specialist who likewise contemplated the intuitive personality through hypnotherapy (the genuine, logical stuff not the senseless diversion mesmerizing you find in stage appears).

Erickson was so proficient at mesmerizing, he built up an approach to address the subconscious mind of other individuals without requiring hypnosis. He could spellbind individuals whenever anyplace in regular discussions. This Erick social strategy for spellbinding got known as conversational hypnosis. This is an extremely useful asset that can be utilized to impact and convince others as well as to enable other individuals to beat fears, restricting convictions, strife and more without their conscious mindfulness. This is particularly valuable when getting crosswise over to individuals who may some way or another be safe on the off chance that they know think adolescent kids who would prefer not to tune in.

NLP and Manipulation

NLP can help you take control of your mind and give you the ability to conquer the world. On the other hand, other people can use it as a form of manipulation in your life. In this section, the book will enlighten you on ways that you can avoid being manipulated and mind-controlled. Having studied the process of NLP over time, I have been able to take note of the people who want to manipulate me into submission. I have developed a strong immune to it.

Be Very Careful About Individuals Mirroring Your Non-Verbal Communication.

In case you're conversing with someone who might be into NLP, and you see that they're sitting in the very same manner as you, or reflecting how you have your hands, test them by causing a couple of developments and checking whether they to accomplish something very similar. Talented NLPer will be greater at veiling this than more up to date ones, however more up to date ones will in every case promptly duplicate a similar development. This is a decent time to call individuals on their crap.

This is cracking humorous to do to stop the NLPer. Particularly in the underlying phases of building a connection, an NLP user will give a fantastically close look in your eyes. You may believe this is because they're seriously intrigued by what you're stating. They are, yet not because they care about your musings: They're watching your eye developments to perceive how you store and access data. In no time, they'll not only have the option to notice when you're telling a lie or causing something to up, they'll additionally have the option to make sense of what parts of your mind you're utilizing when you're talking, which would then be able to lead them to be so enlightened to what you're believing that they nearly seem to be having some sort of mystic knowledge into your deepest contemplations. A cunning hack for this is simply to haphazardly dash your eyes around admire the right, to one side, side to side, down... cause it to appear to be regular, however, do it arbitrarily and with no example. This will get an NLP individual completely crazy since you'll be losing their alignment.

Try Not to Give Anyone a Chance to Touch You

This is entirely clear and to the point. In any case, suppose you're discussing with someone you know is into NLP, and you wind up in an uplifted passionate state perhaps you start chuckling extremely hard or get extremely furious, or something comparative and the individual you're conversing with contacts you while you're in that state. They may, for example, tap you on the shoulder. What simply occurred? They moored you with the goal that later if they need to return you to the state you were simply in, they can touch you in a similar spot. Simply resemble, gracious damnation no you didn't.

Be Careful About the Dubious Language

One of the essential procedures that NLP adopted from Milton Erickson is the utilization of dubious language to instigate. He found that the more ambiguous language is, the more it leads individuals into a stupor because there is less than an individual is obligated to differ with or respond to. On the other hand, increasingly explicit language will remove an individual from the stupor.

Be Careful About the Lenient Language

Statements like "Don't hesitate to unwind." "You're free to test drive this vehicle if you feel like it." "You can stay and let us enjoy this as much as you can imagine." Check the f*k out for this. This was a significant understanding of pre-NLP trance inducers like Erickson: the most ideal approach to get someone to accomplish something, including going into a daze, is by enabling them to give you consent to do as such. Along these lines, talented trance inducers will NEVER order you through and through to accomplish something—for example "Go into a daze." They will make statements like "Don't hesitate to become as loose as you can imagine."

Avoid Gibberish Talk

Crappy statements like "When you unlock this sensation, even more, you'll find yourselves going into the current connection with the tone of your performance evermore." This kind of nonsense is the NLP's stilted dialogue-and-leading process of the main source of income; the hypnotist doesn't say anything, they're just attempting to program the internal mental states and push you wherever they need you to go. Always say "Can you make that far more precise" or "Can you clarify precisely what you mean?" That does two things: One is that it disrupts the whole methodology and also compels the discussion into a particular language, trying to break the use of the vague language that we talked about.

Read Through the Rows

Participants in the NLP can often use hidden or complex definitions of words. For example, "Most important issues are diet, food and sleeping with me, wouldn't you believe?" If you encountered this statement immediately on the ground, it might seem like an obvious point that even without much consideration you would readily agree with. Yeah, diet, exercise, and sleeping are essential things, of course, and it's really good for this individual to be healthier. But what is the meaning built-in? "The most major things are nutrition, diet and lie down with me, don't you think?" Sure, and you committed to it unwittingly. With this, professional NLP persons can be extremely subtle.

Look at Your Target

Be very cautious about zoning all over people with NLP it's an invite to jump in with an unconscious signal. And here is an illustration: A Neuro-linguistic programming user who tried and get me to publish for his website for free discovered that I didn't seem to pay close attention and looked into the range, and then began to just use the methodology mentioned in the previous step to talk about how he would never have to pay for something because news organizations deliver him relatively cheap assessment books and magazines and songs. "Free anything," he started growling at me. "I get it all. By. Fair. "Yes, of course?

Don't Acknowledge Something

If you are guided to make a snap decision about anything and think that you are being directed, escape the situation. Delay for 24 hours, particularly financial related decisions, before making a final decision. You should not allow yourself to be dragged throughout the heat of the moment to make a rational choice. Salespeople are explicitly equipped with NLP methods for engineering purchases of impulses. Don't do that. Move and take control of your conscious mind.

Confide in Your Instincts

And the key rule: believe your instinct if it tells you that someone is messing with you, or you feel uncomfortable about them. Members of the NLP almost seem always "down," shady, or like salespeople of used vehicles. Flee and demand that they show you value while communicating with you not to incorporate NLP strategies.

Chapter 3: Psychology of Manipulation

Manipulation can be negative and positive. However, we hope that the kind of manipulation we give should be of benefit to us in one way or another. Such a way includes enhancing a career or improving our way of life. You should also note that not everyone is of good intentions. Some individuals will manipulate you maliciously leaving you drained and wondering how such an act happened. Manipulation is psychological. In this chapter, we dive into the psychology of manipulation, to see how the manipulators do it.

The specialty of control isn't tied in with causing individuals to do what you need them to do yet rather getting them to need to do what you need them to do. A good book for referencing this is the Art of war by Sun Tzu. It will help you gain proficiency with this. He emphasizes that you should be aware of yourself as well as your enemy. So how would you get individuals to need to do what you need them to? First, you need to get familiar with their actual wants and figure out it toward the objective you need to achieve.

The closer the individual is to you, the simpler it is to control. The closer the individual is to you, the simpler it is to control, very important to take note. In this manner, sentimental accomplices or mates are the best prospects to test your control abilities. What's more, if manipulation gives you a view like it is an awful word, consider it as an influence.

You need to convince individuals. You need to make individuals feel like it was their decision from the beginning. As a rule, men need perfectionism and ladies will in general need completeness. This means that men are normally more effectively convinced by authority and the inner self-related with progress. So, showing vulnerability on whether a man can carefully improve insults the personality that yields progress. With ladies, being adjusted in numerous zones throughout everyday life, particularly with connections of loved ones is a MUST. In this way, choking out time or effect on explicit

connections makes a deep yearning to bring it up. We all need natural balance at a certain level, and we all have to sacrifice and concentrate. Statistically, however, women tend to lean towards equilibrium, while men tend to concentrate on perfectionism.
You should think about how to impact other people's emotions. Since simply like Maya Angelou always said, individuals may overlook what you did or said however they will recall how you made them feel. Likewise, the vast majority need to control over the present moment. Nonetheless, the genuine craft of control is truly adoring the long game. Persistence is temperance. Thus, to how experts make their "craft" looks simple, you need to make the enticement feel and stream easily. It requires some investment, and tolerance for you to rationally beat your psychological hindrances and get your outlook right.

Something that mentally hurt controllers in this procedure is the lack of understanding and moving with the compelling force of nature. Much the same as a rock moving down the slope, you need to let gravity (nature) have a pull of you. Try not to compel or conflict with natural force. At the point when it downpours, we adjust by having an umbrella or coat. At the point when it is hot, we change our wearing style to the light layers of apparel due to the heat. Fundamentally, I'm stating don't be rigid and change following what is. How would you measure for delusion?

Two different ways: making the best decision in an inappropriate request is yet an inappropriate thing otherwise known as, miss prioritization of needs and having desires for yield from a piece of inappropriate information. So, with individuals, we need to realize their character type, how they react to specific conditions, and what are their limits.

So, here's the great part. The psychological structures are off the path. So how precisely you get them to accomplish the thing? To start with, you need to take lead with the benefit. Individuals love the arrival of the remuneration. By what method can the "thing" you need them to do be of profit? Presently, don't let them know legitimately to do it. Studies have appeared, 90% of the time, individuals despise being determined what to do.

Rather, you assist them with arriving at the same resolution all alone "way". Individuals love feeling like it was their thought (not yours). So, let them possess it. The main genuine crucial step is appending the "reward" or advantage to the thing. In such a case that individuals don't see how something benefits them, they will probably never do it.

Additionally, taking a closer look at connections of what individuals that accomplish the thing you need to impart do just as the "thing". For instance, if you need to convince somebody to get more fit and bringing up a "diet" is hard. Take a stab at discussing improved skin composition which is by implication related to incredible eating regimens.

You can lead individuals to the water source, however now and then you can't cause them to drink. So, all things considered, make them feel the thirst. Interest wins! Get the individual inquisitive about themes and you'll get nature working for you, like a stone moving down the slope because of gravity. Never ignore every logical law, simply stream with it. When you have effectively succeeded in manipulation, never uncover yourself since it will ignore loving and adoring inclination and individuals will cut you off. You don't need that. Keep up cognizance of how you are making them feel and attempt to control, "convince", generally advantageous, do not be malicious.

How to Note Manipulators

Most of the time, you maybe be played into getting a notice of the manipulators. In their minds, it is their wish that you will note know them so that they can succeed in manipulating your mind.

However, I have widely done research and noted the techniques that manipulators like to pull to avoid being noted. Notwithstanding, it's imperative to perceive these practices in circumstances where your privileges, interests, and wellbeing are in question.

- **The Physical Space Advantages**
  A manipulative individual may demand your meeting and associate in a physical room where the person in question can practice more strength and control. This can be the controller's office, home, vehicle, or different spaces where he feels possession and recognition (and where you need them).

- **Gives You a Chance to Speak First to Establish Your Baseline and Look for Weaknesses**
  Numerous sales reps do this when they prospect you. By asking you general and examining inquiries, they build up a benchmark about your reasoning and conduct, from which they would then be able to assess your qualities and shortcomings. This sort of addressing with concealed motivation can likewise happen in the working environment or in close to home connections.

- **Control of Facts**
  This involves Lying, reason making, deceitfulness, censuring the unfortunate casualty for causing their exploitation. It also involves disfigurement of reality, vital exposure or retaining of key data, distortion, modest representation of the truth and uneven predisposition of issue.

- **Overpower You with Facts and Statistics**
  A few people appreciate "scholarly tormenting" by venturing to be the master and most proficient in specific zones. They exploit you by forcing asserted certainties, measurements, and other information you may think minimal about. This can occur in deals and monetary circumstances, in proficient dialogs and dealings, just as in social and social contentions. By assuming master control over you, the controller would like to push through her or his motivation all the more convincingly. A few people utilize this system

for no other explanation than to feel a feeling of scholarly predominance.

- **Overpower You with Procedures and Red Tape**
  Certain individuals use organization desk work, techniques, laws and by-laws, advisory groups, and different detours to keep up their position and power while making your life progressively troublesome. This system can likewise be utilized to postpone actuality finding and truth chasing, shroud defects and shortcomings, and sidestep examination.

- **Raising Their Voice and Displaying Negative Emotions**
  A few people speak more loudly during talks as a type of forceful control. The suspicion might be that on the off chance that they anticipate their voice boisterously enough, or show negative feelings, you'll submit to their pressure and give them what they need. The forceful voice is much of the time joined with solid non-verbal communication, for example, standing or energized signals to expand sway.

- **Negative Surprises**
  A few people use contrary amazements to put you wobbly and increase a mental favorable position. This can go from low balling in an exchange circumstance, to an unexpected calling that she or he won't have the option to come through and convey somehow or another. Regularly, the startling negative data comes abruptly, so you have a brief period to get ready and counter their turn. The controller may request extra concessions from you to keep working with you.

- **Giving You Little or No Time to Decide**
  This is a typical deal and arrangement strategy, where the controller puts pressure on you to prepare a choice before you're. By applying strain and control onto you,

it is trusted that you will "split" and yield to the attacker's requests.

- **Negative Humor Designed to Poke at Your Weaknesses and Disempower You**
  A few controllers like to make basic comments, frequently masked as silliness or mockery, to cause you to appear to be second rate and less secure. Models can incorporate an assortment of remarks running from your appearance, to your more seasoned model advanced mobile phone, to your experience and qualifications, to the way that you strolled quickly late and exhausted. By making you look terrible, and getting you to feel awful, the attacker would like to force mental predominance over you.

- **Reliably Judge and Criticize You to Make You Feel Inadequate**
  Particular from the past conduct where negative cleverness is utilized as a spread, here the controller out and out singles out you. By always underestimating, mocking, and rejecting you, she or he keeps you reeling and keeps up her predominance. The attacker purposely cultivates the feeling that there's continually some kind of problem with you, and that regardless of how hard you attempt, you are lacking and will never be sufficient. Altogether, the controller centers around the negative without giving authentic and valuable arrangements or offering significant approaches to help.

- **The Silent Treatment**
  By purposely not reacting to your sensible calls, instant messages, messages, or different request, the controller presumes control by making you pause, and means to place uncertainty and vulnerability in your brain. The quiet treatment is a head game where quietness is utilized as a type of influence.

- **Imagine Ignorance**

  This is a great "playing stupid" strategy. By imagining she or he doesn't comprehend what you need, or what you need her to do, the controller/inactive forceful makes you take on what is her obligation and gets you to start to perspire. A few youngsters utilize this strategy to the postponement, slow down, and control grown-ups into accomplishing for them what they would prefer not to do. Some adults utilize this strategy too when they have something to cover up or commitment, they wish to maintain a strategic distance from.

- **Blame Baiting**

  This is made up of unreasonable accusing, focusing on the beneficiary's weakness, considering another answerable for the controller's satisfaction and achievement, or misery and disappointments. By focusing on the beneficiary's passionate shortcomings and weakness, the controller constrains the beneficiary into surrendering nonsensical demands and requests.

- **Victimhood**

  Models: Exaggerated or envisioned individual issues. Misrepresented or envisioned medical problems. Reliance. Codependency. Intentional fragility to evoke compassion and support. Playing frail, weak, or saint. The motivation behind manipulative victimhood is frequently to abuse the beneficiary's great will, feeling of remorse, feeling of obligation and commitment, or defensive and supporting sense, to extricate nonsensical advantages and concessions.

Manipulative Relationships

Even though you might be more acquainted by the most common causes of an unhappy relationship, such as a spouse that pressures you to wear in some way or prevents you from having to interact with friends and family, there are many other signs that your relationship is obsessive, manipulative, or unhealthy. Have a read, and understand: believe in your gut, and let no one talk to you in a love model which doesn't sound right for you. Love should feel happy, not overpowering, frightening, or exhausting and having a partner should make you feel better, not sadder.

Signs That You Should Take Note of in an Emotionally Abusive Relationship

When you are in a toxic relationship, most of the time you may not notice. Rather, the people outside can see clearly that your relationship is bad. This is because love may have blinded it all such that you may not be able to recognize the red flags. Here are some of the things you should look out for to examine a toxic and manipulative relationship.

- **You Feel Guilty When You Spend Time with Friends**

At the point when we envision somebody attempting to cut their lover off from their emotionally supportive network, we for the most part picture something sensational, similar to the despicable spouse. In any case, all things considered, controlling partners, for the most part, disconnect you from your close community in a considerably more inconspicuous manner.

As opposed to viciously denying you from reaching your companions or family, a controlling partner may just tenderly push you away from them. They make you feel very bad about having a real-life to live outside of the relationship. The vast majority don't care to feel along these lines so you may begin to adjust how you act, where you go, who you spend time with, and so forth., to abstain from feeling this remorseful. To start with, this feels your partner is truly into you so it's basic not to understand that it's going on, particularly if you have a background marked by being treated this way while growing up from childhood.

Possibly your partner frowns each time you go out with your close friends until you start avoiding their lunch and weekend invites just to save yourself the pressure. Possibly your husband or wife makes negative remarks about your friends until you begin to accept that the reactions are valid. Possibly your public activity spins around a leisure activity that is your favorite, however, your new partner thinks your side interest is crazy and makes you dumb. They ridicule you for it until you give it up. This conduct can take a wide range of structures; however, it generally has a similar objective: stressing or cutting off your associations with different individuals you are close to until you feel that your lover is the main individual you have on the planet.

Step By Step Instructions to Tell It Apart From Healthy Behavior

Though a significant number of us have encountered the honeymoon frame at an opportune time in another relationship where all you need to do is invest energy with your new partner and regularly disregard your friends all the while, this is altogether different. Half a month or long stretches of focusing on your new love can be typical and fun. Yet, if your accomplice effectively urges you to split away from your friends, that is an undesirable relationship.

- **They Condemn Lots of Different Tasks That You Do**

A critique from a manipulating spouse might not even look like a critical analysis that may be lined up in "helpful" language that means that your spouse is just attempting to help you. Yet it is important to take note if it doesn't feel right. It is erosive to attack. Criticism implies that there is some kind of appearance or character trait in us, and that's why critique is so harmful. Anyone who cherishes and embraces us for our real self and not trying to make people feel smaller or much less than, may want or need us to enhance a tradition, but they love who we are as an individual.

How Do You Differentiate It From A Healthy Behavior

Whereas many partners sometimes condemn one another, when the criticism is constant and implies that you are unable to make good choices through your own, this is a warning sign? And whether you are speaking of your job, peers, or wardrobe, it's dangerous to think that your partner knows better than you do. Their words aren't really about achieving your goals they are all about weakening your choice-making ability and taking action alone.

- **Lack of Trust**

Indeed, even individuals who are profoundly in love are permitted to have some space of themselves. Furthermore, a partner who will not recognize this and claims that individuals who care about one another don't keep their writings or messages private, or will enable their accomplice to read through their journal isn't being sentimental. They're being controlling. Your partner doesn't reserve the option to browse your email or messages or approach your online life passwords since they state they're "apprehensive" you may cheat, or because they guarantee that individuals who are infatuated don't have insider facts. There's a distinction between "having insider facts" and having a presence free of your partner and you don't need to surrender the latter to be in a love relationship.

Trust is a basic piece of any sound relationship yet it very well may be utilized as a device to cause a partner to demonstrate their dependability and love. If your partner has to know where you are every time but does not expect you to have the same privilege, then there is an imbalance in the relationship. In a perfect world, trust streams unreservedly the two different ways.

Instructions To Tell It Apart From Healthy Behavior

Now and again, genuine couples who are recouping from an episode of cheating will permit the undermined accomplice access to the partners' writings and messages for a constrained timeframe as a type of responsibility. However, if this isn't an arrangement that you have explicitly worked out with your accomplice in this unique situation and ideally with the assistance of an advocate, it isn't right.

- **They Always Talk About Protecting You**

Many of us have had shitty things happening in our lives. There have been enough crappy things that even the idea of a hero sitting on a white horse or fixie bike and saving us all from the consequences for the rest of our life can sound very, really enticing. So, respecting somebody usually includes defensive feelings. Usually, we want to bend down to keep in any way the individuals we love from enduring. Yet think twice if the aid ideas of your partner include protecting you from taking responsibility for your actions and enjoying your own life. A manipulating partner could develop a sense of false consciousness, i.e. you simply don't care for yourself without your spouse. This can also occur in terms of money. A spouse who "aims to protect" you by seizing control in your chaotic savings account, driving back a friend you have been arguing with, or keeping a tight track on how you are and what you are doing at all times doesn't look out for you, they're attempting to make you reliant on them.

How To Tell It Apart From A Good Behavior

A good partner knows they can't "protect" you from life's ugliness and they can just love you and stand by you. If you are in an economic mess, a supportive partner can buy you financial planning books, help you to find money management tools, recommend that you take a financial planning course, or offer to help you get through your unopened credit card bills backlog while offering emotional help. Yet, once you pay off your credit card debt, they didn't take your bank password, manage your bills, and give you an allowance. A happy spouse will be able to offer all kinds of support; however, he knows you have to deal with your issues in the end.

- **You Start Questioning Yourself**

A manipulating partner will sometimes never avoid trying to cut you off from your support system they might also try to cut you off from your sense of reality. There is a common technique for manipulating the relationship called gaslighting, in which your partner messes with your sense of reality to make you question your judgment. Imagine you found your friend on social media snooping your direct messages and you're questioning them and they are denying it. They might say that you're thinking it, that it may have been someone else, etc., and as a consequence, you're starting to doubt yourself in and starting to think you've been insane to doubt your spouse. This is even though you have your spouse is the one in the wrong. A partner in gaslighting can say that events you know have never occurred. For instance, if you're bringing up a battle you two had last Tuesday, they might deny you've even been apart that day. In other ways, a gaslighting partner can also screw with your conceptualization of reality like throwing out your ownership and denying it, or persuading you that your supervisor has been quiet recently because they are planning to lay you off. How to differentiate It from Good Behavior: Our friends are required to think about something from time to time. If your spouse casts out an empty box that you have had in the house, then legally tends to forget that it occurred when you ask about it some weeks later. But if you see a routine especially when it comes to your spouse rejecting experiences that you two have or remarks that you know they've made you should recognize.

Anyone can fall into a controlling relationship, no matter how intelligent, clever, or social justice warrior you are and recognizing that you are in this does not render you any less intelligent, smart, or social justice warrior. Do not feel silly because you ought to have seen the red flags. Marital power often creeps on us, and we soon won't see them for everything they are until we're strong in them. But if any of this sounds like your life, keep in mind: that it is not your fault, and with that, you don't have to live. Despite what you've been told by your wife, other people care for you, some like you, and others want to be in a relationship with you.

How to Control Manipulative Relationships

You must become aware that you are in a negative environment that hinders your progress in personal life. You should note that all-round success is necessary. If things are not going well in your house, you will not be able to be of influence out there. It may be hard to control an already advanced manipulative relationship. However, it is never too late to save yourself from agony. You are human with a right to live a full, happy life away from abuse.

Get to Know Your Basic Rights

The absolute most significant rule when you're managing a mentally manipulative individual is to know your privileges and perceive when they are being taken advantage of. When you don't hurt others, you are allowed to protect yourself and stand for your rights. Then again, if you carry damage to other people, you may relinquish these rights. Below are the basics of our rights;

You have the right:

- To be treated with respectfully
- To express your sentiments, assessments, and needs.
- To set your very own needs.
- To state "no" without feeling regretful.
- To receive exactly what you paid for.
- To have suppositions not the same as others.
- To deal with and shield yourself from being undermined physically, rationally or emotions abuse.
- To make your very own upbeat and sound life.

These major human rights speak to your limits. The general public is filled with individuals who do not regard these rights. Mental controllers, specifically, need to deny you of your privileges so they can control and exploit you. Yet, you have the power and good position to proclaim that it is you, not the controller, who's responsible for your life.

Stay Away

One approach to identify a controller is to check whether an individual demonstrates various faces before various individuals and in various circumstances. While we all have a level of this sort of social separation, some mental controllers will in general constantly stay in boundaries, being exceptionally amenable to one individual and inconsiderate to another—or vulnerable one minute and wildly forceful the following. At the point when you watch this sort of conduct from a person all the time, keep a solid separation, and abstain from connecting with the individual except if you need to. As referenced before, the purposes of ceaseless mental control are intricate and profound situated. It isn't your business to change or spare them.

Dodge Self-Blame

Since the controller plans to search for and misuse your shortcomings, it is reasonable that you may feel lacking, or even reprimand yourself for not fulfilling the controller. In these circumstances, recollect that you are not the issue; you're just being controlled to feel terrible about yourself, with the goal that you're bound to give up your capacity and rights. Think about your association with the controller, and pose the accompanying inquiries:

- Am I being treated with real regard?
- Are this current individual's desires and requests of me sensible?
- Is the giving in this relationship fundamentally one way or two different ways?
- At last, do I like myself in this relationship?
- Your responses to these inquiries give you significant pieces of information about whether the "issue" in the relationship is with you or the other individual.
- Put the Focus on Them by Asking Probing Questions

Mental controllers will make demands (or requests) of you. These "offers" regularly cause you to make a special effort to address their issues. At the point when you hear an absurd sale, it's occasionally valuable to return the attention on the controller by asking a couple of testing inquiries, to check whether she or he has enough mindfulness to perceive the disparity of their plan. For instance:

- Does this appear to be sensible to you?
- Does what you need from me sound reasonable?
- Do I have an opinion on this?
- Is it accurate to say that you are asking me or letting me know?
- All in all, what do I escape this?
- Is it true that you are truly anticipating this from me?

At the point when you pose such inquiries, you're setting up a reflection, so the controller can see the genuine idea of their ploy. If the controller has a level of mindfulness, the person will probably pull back the interest and back down. Also, obsessive controllers, for example, a narcissist will reject your inquiries and demand getting their direction. If this happens, apply thoughts from the accompanying tips to keep your capacity, and end the control.

Use Time in the Best Way

In regards to undue demands, the manipulator may sometimes also expect an immediate response by you to optimize their strain and power towards you in the circumstance. The salespeople call it' closing the agreement. In these instances, instead of reacting instantly to the manipulator's query, consider using the time to your benefit and trying to distance oneself from your partner's immediate control. You can practice governance in the circumstance by merely saying:

I will give it a thought.' Imagine how effective just those few phrases are of a buyer to a salesman, or maybe from a passionate point of view to an enthusiastic opponent, or from yourself to a manipulator. Spend the time that you need to assess the advantages and disadvantages of the scenario, and recognize if you want to bargain a fairer agreement, or if you are safer off by saying "no," which brings to our next point:
Learn how to say' no' diplomatically, but strongly Being able to just say' no in a diplomatic way, but staunchly, is to learn the art of interaction. Efficiently expressed, it enables you to hold your ground while retaining a positive working relationship. Note

that your basic human rights also include the right to establish your own goals, the right to say' no' without feeling guilty, and the right to use your own healthy and happy life.

Face Up the Bullies, Efficiently

The mental manipulator is also a bully if he or she frightens or hurts another human. The most essential thing to remember about trouble makers is that they would choose who they see as fragile, so long as you stay timid and compatible, you put yourself in danger. But so many abusers are also cowards within. Once their goals start to show their strength and fight for their rights, they will often come straight back. This is true in school playgrounds, as well as in the home and office settings. Studies show, on an empathetic level, that many bullies themselves are victims of violence. That in no way justifies the actions of abuse, but it may allow you to view the dictator in a more calm and positive light: It is said that If people don't like themselves so much, they have to make up for it. The classic killer was the first recipient. When facing menaces, make certain to put yourself in a position where you can securely ensure yourself, regardless of whether it's standing tall all alone, having other individuals present to observe and support, or keeping a paper trail of the domineering bully's wrongful conduct. In instances of physical, verbal, or psychological mistreatment, counsel with directing, lawful, law implementation, or regulatory experts. It's critical to face the bullies, and you don't need to do it alone.

Set Consequences

At the point when a mental controller demands to disregard your limits, and won't take "no" for an answer, send outcome. The capacity to recognize and attest to the impact is one of the most significant abilities you can use to remain down a troublesome individual. Viably enunciated, the result offers a pause to the manipulative person and forces her or him to move from infringement to high regard.

Chapter 4: Mind Controls

What are Mind Controls?

Mind control is a concept that has long been fascinating individuals. The press and films have shared stories regarding groups of individuals who were brainwashed or hypnotized to do stuff they never would have performed otherwise. This comes as a result of not nurturing your NLP to take note when you are being manipulated. There are people on all sides of the matter; some claim that there's no such thing as mind control, and it is all composed, while some believe they can be controlled at any time by mind control. For several years now, the concept of mind control has been there. Individuals were both intrigued and terrified about what would occur if anyone could manipulate their thoughts and have them do something against their own will. While many different kinds of mind manipulation can be used to manipulate the intended target, the most widely known are five. They include; Brainwashing, hypnosis, coercion, deceit, and persuasion. We are going to address this below.

Brainwashing

Brainwashing is the primary sort of mind control to talk about. It is essentially the process where somebody will be plotted to relinquish convictions that they had previously believed in to take up new goals and values as well as beliefs. There are a ton of ways this is done possible even though not every one of them will be viewed as a bad way. For instance, if you are from an African nation and, at that point relocate to America, you will frequently be compelled to change your qualities and beliefs to fit in with the new culture and environment.

Then again, those in thoughts or when another tyrant government is assuming control over, they will regularly experience the way toward indoctrinating to persuade residents to come along with peace. Numerous individuals have misguided judgments of what mentally programming is. A few people have progressively suspicious thoughts regarding the work on including mind control gadgets that are supported by the administration and that are believed to be effectively turned on like a remote control.

However, some doubters don't accept that brainwashing is conceivable at all and that any individual who believes it has happened is telling a lie. Generally, the act of brainwashing will arrive someplace in these two thoughts. Through the act of brainwashing, the subject will be persuaded to change their convictions about something through a blend of various strategies. There isn't only one methodology that can be utilized during this procedure so it tends to be hard to place the training into a perfect little space. Generally, the victim will be isolated from everything that they know. From that point, they will be separated into a passionate state that makes them powerless before the new ideas are presented. As the subject assimilates this new data, they will be remunerated for communicating thoughts and ideas which oblige these new thoughts. The compensating is the thing that will be utilized to strengthen the brainwashing that is happening. Individuals have been utilizing these strategies for quite a while. For instance, in a verifiable setting, the individuals who were detainees of wars were regularly broken down before being convinced to changes sides. Probably the most effective instances of these would bring about the detainee turning into a very intense proselyte to the new side.

These practices were very new in the first place and would frequently be authorized relying upon who was in control. After some time, the word brainwashing was created and some more strategies were acquainted all together with make the training increasingly general. The more up to date procedures would depend on the field of psychology since a large number of those thoughts were utilized to exhibit how individuals may alter their perspectives through influence. Numerous means accompany the brainwashing procedure. It isn't something that is going to simply transpire when you stroll down the road and furthermore, converse with somebody that you have quite recently met.

For one thing, one of the fundamental prerequisites that accompany mentally programming being effective is that the subject must be kept in detachment. If the subject can be around other individuals and impacts, they will figure out how to think as an individual and the indoctrinating won't be compelling by any stretch of the imagination.

Hypnosis

Hypnosis is a process that occurs naturally, we continually slip into and out of hypnotic states. The use of hypnosis to just awaken individuals out of unhealthy conditions can be as effective as bringing them into better states.

Hypnosis and relaxation proceed to unconscious states which have been used since the beginning of civilization to make us calm, concentrate and enhance well-being and innovation. Mindfulness and hypnosis have many comparisons. The key difference is mindfulness is about accepting and just being available to anything that happens, while hypnosis is more directional, it's about leading us or others to almost anything healthier. The ideal situation is to fully appreciate what we have already and strive toward anything good. It is important to note that the NLP approach is enhanced by hypnosis.

Hypnosis Concepts

The strength of uncertainty. If we only give our customers a framework with little or no material, they will often fill in the gaps in the framework at such a time with one of the most valuable content for them. Often space is more helpful than offering them the (or indeed our) answer. Saying' You can choose to take the correct action you know' is ambiguous.

Therefore, refusing outright is very hard and this helps the customer to apply the terms to what matters to them.

1. The secret is rhythm, tone, and movement. We bathe in sound for our customers.
2. Disrupts in surprise and sequence are useful, as long as we use them to proceed productively.

3. By reference to anything that is indisputable valid in their universe, speed and then leads can also be used. If they support what we say, we can be more successful in taking them anywhere.

4. Something that presupposes a hypnotic state also contributes to it. Promote all activity that facilitates the hypnosis of your customer. When you notice symptoms like faster breathing, eyes flapping, increased muscles and skin flaccidity, glassy eyes, and bottom lip getting redder say' That's wrong' or' That's great.'

Utilization

We can use whatever happens. For example, if a car alarm goes off as you support your customer relax profoundly, you can integrate this disruption and say:' you can hear an alarm, and as the alarm is quieter as the car goes further, you can concentrate more on what matters to you.'

Fractionation. Many small woven fragments work incredibly well during a regular conversation. Little more than often, it operates because it can make customers uneasy too soon. Leave them to want more.

1. Get in touch, get into a trance, and the customer is going to follow.

2. It could also be called a deep hypnotic condition as a normal state of complete relationship / deep learning. We can sometimes substitute' or' with' and' in a hypnotic trance.

Coercion

Coercive psychological structures are behavioral modification initiatives that use coercive psychological pressure to induce a philosophy or established set of values, thoughts, perceptions, or habits to be acquired and adopted. The basic technique used in these programs ' administrators is to routinely pick, list, and organize several various types of coercive control, distress, and anxiety-producing strategies over time. The subject is forced to conform in such a system in a couple of small "imaginary" phases. That small step is intended to be subtle enough so that the participants do not perceive the changes in themselves or assess the oppressive nature of the procedures being utilized.

Till much later, if ever, the targets of these techniques will not become informed of the coercive psychological programs secret administrative intent. Generally, these techniques were implemented by well-intentioned but misled friends of the victim in a group situation. In known oppositional situations, this keeps the victim from having to put up the ego defensive capabilities that we usually preserve. The oppressive psychological power of these programs, other than any claim to reasoned judgment, attempts to suppress the ability to think critically and free will of the victim. Victims slowly reduce their ability to practice proper consent and make sensible choices.

Their critical thinking, defenses, cognitive processes, beliefs, concepts, behaviors, actions, and capacity to reason are compromised by a technical mechanism rather than by actual free choice, rationality, or the intrinsic validity or importance of the proposed ideas or proposals. How are they going to work?

The strategies used to establish excessive social and psychological control drop into 7 major categories, often through methods containing stress and anxiety.

- **Strategy 1:** Improve suggestibility and "soften" individuals by different hypnotic or other suggestibility increasing techniques such as prolonged video, visual, verbal, or tactile fixation exercises, Excessive accurate repetition of routine activity, Sleep restriction and/or Nutritional restriction.

- **Strategy 2:** Develop power over most of the social context, time, and links of welfare support of the individual through a scheme of many rewards and punishments. The promotion of isolation and loneliness. There is a shortened direct communication with loved ones, as is interaction with people who don't share perceptions endorsed by the group. It encourages financial and other community dependencies.

- **Strategy 3:** Prohibit disconfirmation in group interaction of facts or un-supporting views. There are guidelines for appropriate subjects to be shared with outsiders. There is a high level of control over the interaction. Typically, the phrase "in-group" is created.

- **Strategy 4:** Cause the individual re-to to assess the most focal parts of their experience of self and earlier lead in negative manners. Endeavors are intended to destabilize and undermine the subject's fundamental cognizance, reality mindfulness, world view, enthusiastic control, and safeguard components. The subject is guided to reinterpret their life's history and embrace another adaptation of causality.

- **Strategy 5:** Make a feeling of frailty by exposing the individual to exceptional and continuous activities and circumstances which undermine the individual's trust in himself and his overall judgment.

- **Strategy 6:** Make solid aversive passionate feelings of excitement in the subject by utilization of nonphysical disciplines, for example, serious mortification, loss of benefits, social disconnection, economic wellbeing changes, exceptional blame, tension, control, and different methods.

- **Strategy 7:** Threaten the individual with the power of gathering endorsed common mental dangers. For instance, it might be proposed or suggested that inability to receive the affirmed disposition, conviction or subsequent conduct will prompt serious discipline or desperate results, for example, physical or psychological sickness, the return of an earlier physical disease, sedate reliance, financial breakdown, social disappointment, separate, deterioration, inability to discover a mate, and so on.

Such psychological coercion techniques are implemented so strongly that it prevents the ability of the victim to make sensible or independent decisions. Victims are unable to undertake the ordinary, prudent, or rational choices which they most probably or would usually have made if these orchestrated technological processes did not exploit them unknowingly. The combined effect of such procedures can be a means of disproportionate influence which is even more powerful than pain, coercion, abuse or use of physical violence and physical and legal intimidation.

How Coercion Differs from the Rest Types of Influence

Coercive mental frameworks are recognized from social learning or quiet influenced by the particular conditions under which they are led. These conditions incorporate the sort and number of coercive mental strategies utilized, the seriousness of natural and relational control, and the measure of mental power utilized to stifle specific undesirable practices and to prepare wanted practices.

Coercive power is customarily pictured in physical terms. In this structure, it is effectively quantifiable, obvious, and unambiguous. Coercive mental power sadly has not been so natural to see and characterize. The law has been in front of the physical sciences in that it has permitted that compulsion need not include physical power. It has perceived that an individual can be compromised and forced mentally by what the person seems to be perilous, not really by that which is hazardous.

Law has perceived that even compromised activity need not be physical. Dangers of financial misfortune, social shunning, and scorn, in addition to other things, are altogether perceived by law, in shifting settings, as coercive mental powers.

The Downside of Coercive Psychological System

The most basic principles of fundamental human rights are violated by coercive psychological processes. We violate the rights of persons protected by the First Amendment to the Constitution of the United States and supported by many statements of principle all over the world.

Through misleading, threatening and trying to silence their targets, those who benefit from these schemes avoid scrutiny and conviction for conduct regarded as dangerous and illegal in most countries such as fraud, unlawful imprisonment, undue influence, involuntary servitude, deliberate emotional distress infliction, outrageous behavior, and other grueling actions.

Deceit

Double-dealing alludes to the demonstration enormous or little, savage or sort of making somebody think something that is false. Indeed, even the most legitimate individuals practice misdirection, with different examinations demonstrating that the normal individual lies a few times each day. A portion of those falsehoods is huge such as "I've never undermined you!" however more regularly, they are harmless embellishments "That dress looks fine," that is conveyed to keep away from awkward circumstances to somebody's emotions. Deception isn't constantly an outward-confronting act. There are additionally the untruths individuals let themselves know, for reasons running from the solid support of confidence to genuine hallucinations outside their ability to control. While deceiving oneself is commonly seen as hurtful, a few specialists contend that there are particular sorts of self-misdirection like trusting one can achieve a troublesome objective regardless of whether proof exists in actuality that can positively affect by and large prosperity. Trust is the bedrock of public activity at all levels, from sentiment and child-rearing to national government and universal settlements. Deception consistently undermines it.

Scientists have looked for approaches to completely identify when somebody is lying. Extraordinary compared to other known strategies, the polygraph test, depends on the hypothesis that lying changes ordinary psychophysiological designs that can be identified by delicate hardware. Albeit well known in wrongdoing shows and motion pictures, the test has for some time been questionable, with no proof that there are authoritative changes in physiology. Proof proposes that those with certain mental issues like Antisocial Personality Disorder can't be precisely estimated by a polygraph or other normally utilized untruth location techniques.

Numerous specialists suggest that liars uncover themselves in "tells," major and minor changes in non-verbal communication or outward appearances. In any case, proof shows that perceptible indications of lying can be inconsistent, and misleading identification even by analysts is no more prominent than a possibility.

Identification of misdirection is basic for law requirement, and the quest for solid techniques is regularly progressing. Many invested individuals have moved their concentrate away from outward indications of deceiving the utilization of meeting methods that uncover lying. The research proposes that, in vital circumstances, the number of words, the sort of words, the redundancy of words would all be able to help prepared questioners distinguish duplicity.

Why People Tell Lies

Nobody likes being misled, and when public figures are trapped in a lying scandal, it can turn into a significant embarrassment. In any case, while numerous individuals pride themselves on their circumspect trustworthiness and attempt to remove themselves from people who are progressively alright with deceptions in all actuality everybody lies, for an assortment of reasons. Truth be told, a few specialists recommend that a specific measure of duplicity might be fundamental for keeping up a sound, working society. The conventional investigation of misdirection was before the area of ethicists and scholars, yet more as of late, analysts have directed their concentration toward why individuals lie, and the conditions that make them bound to do as such.

Persuasion

Working environment persuasion or other environments include persuading others to pursue a plan of action, commit to an agreement, or make a purchase or service. In general, employers prefer persuasive skills in their workers because they can affect so many facets of the organization, leading to increased profitability. Persuasion is based on six principles. Let us look into what they have to increase your productivity and enhance your career and general life.

Persuasive skills are needed if project participants are to be affected. These may include clients, co-workers, present or current and potential bosses, business partners, subordinates, contributors, revenue sources, magistrates, prosecutors, customers, voters, and potential employees.

The Process of Persuasion

Persuasion does not just happen instantly, it takes some effort. The following is the procedure you should take. Surveying the inclinations, needs, and predispositions of a focused individual or gathering.

Convincing others is most effectively achieved by clarifying how a proposition you are recommending would be commonly valuable to the client. In the business area, this phase of the influence procedure is classified as "consultative prompting," during which a salesman who has skills will initially get some information about their client's likes and preferences or necessities before exhibiting a solution. For example; Composing the content for a phone gathering pledges contribute request to fund-raise for an association of charity.

Building a Relationship with Specific Partners

When you've set up what precisely target partners need, you can utilize this data to start to assemble compatibility with them. Remember that, in many workplaces, building affinity is a ceaseless procedure. For example, much after you have accomplished group purchase in for an assignment, you should keep on building compatibility for future coordinated efforts by commending colleagues, all through the periods of the venture's culmination, for work well-done. For example; Asking a client how her child or little girl is faring in school as a feature of building an association with the students and their family.

Plainly Articulating the Advantages of the Acceptance of a Proposed Agenda

Having invested some energy in the primary phase of influence posting the necessities of your partners that you can supply, you'll be well-prepared to portray to them the advantages of receiving your proposition. In deals, this stage is some of the time depicted as making an "esteem included" suggestion – however concentrating on the advantages of your offering is a decent technique regardless of what the conditions. For example; Urging a patient to focus on building a much healthy way of life.

Effectively Tuning in to the Worries of Partners and Revealing Any Issues to a Made Proposal

At the point when you are in the place where you have to convince others about a game-plan, it's ideal to anticipate and be set up for potential complaints (there is consistently somebody who will attempt to toss a spanner into the works!). Complaints will be simpler to survive on the off chance that you've endeavored to tune in to and regard other individuals' worries about another task or adventure. For example; You can meet with a staff part to survey their response to a proposed rebuilding of the organization.

Introducing Contradictions to Overcome Any Complaints

This is one of the most testing phases of the persuasion procedure. If you've precisely anticipated potential protests, however, you ought to have the option to go through contradictions convincingly.

For example; Arranging a compensation increment or extra get-away time.

Perceiving Any Real Confinements to a Proposal

Individuals are commonly increasingly agreeable to influence and arrangement if you show straightforwardness in the process just as your ability to perceive legitimate issues with your arrangement. For example; Agreeing that your group should work with a little spending plan than you'd sought after.

Altering a Proposition as Required to Discover a Shared View with Partners

Most recommendations are they some business deal activities or work environment dealings require bargain. It's great to know early which components of a proposition you can be adaptable about. For example; Leading association exchanges for more significant compensations or improved benefits.

Explaining the Conditions of Any Last Understanding

Nobody needs to return and start the influence procedure once more because a partner hasn't comprehended the last terms of an understanding or agreement. Lucidity in clarifying the foreseen outcomes of an understanding is essential. For example; Instructing another worker about conditions for their procuring and/or end.

Directing follow-up to decide whether any partners have to wait for questions about a proposition

Not exclusively subsequent meet-ups with partners assemble compatibility, yet they likewise help you to follow the accomplishment of a settled upon an adventure. Structuring and dispersing client input reviews.

Principles of Persuasion

Liking

To like this to be manipulated by people is to look for ways to become like you. Are you fond of golf? I, too. Do you like soccer? I, too. While these are often authentic, they are not occasionally.

Preference is consistent sufficiently to point out the difference that it sometimes bears. Someone could ask, "Would you like your site to have more guests?" They do not simply pursue an association with you (as in Liking) but instead pursue consistency. For sure, you'll answer yes, and in principle, when you're offered service or product later, you'll have a harder time to back up that assertion.

Reciprocity

One of the most essential standards of impact is to just give what you need to get. At the end of the day, doing directly by others is a decent method to get others to do likewise for you. This thought of correspondence is an amazing one.

There are two or three different ways to have this correspondence work for you. Giving others little blessings, approaching others with deference, and doing favors for those out of luck, are everything that can win you focuses on different people. So, a decent approach is to consistently help other people and be caring when you have the chance since no one can tell how it might assist you with bringing down the line. Besides, it is these little demonstrations of thoughtfulness that will be recollected and prove to be useful when you're needing some help yourself.

Consistency

The rule of consistency depends on the intensity of dynamic, public, and deliberate responsibilities, which results in individuals adhering to their promise. We should stroll through these necessities in somewhat more detail. The initial segment is a functioning duty. By dynamic, Cialdini implies something that is composed. Having individuals state they will accomplish something is a beginning, however, when they effectively focus on it, they're substantially more liable to finish.

The following step is making it open. At the point when other's observer this dedication, it adds a degree of responsibility to the announcement. Also, nobody needs to backpedal on their promise.

At long last, it must be deliberate. If you power somebody to make a functioning, open responsibility that they didn't settle on themselves, you've achieved nothing.

So how would you utilize this? When you've convinced somebody to accomplish something, get them to make these sorts of duties to execute the standard of consistency and guarantee there is a genuine responsibility to their words.

Social Proof

Individuals depend on meaningful gestures from others on the best way to think, feel, and act by and large. What's more, any individuals, yet peers. Individuals they accept are like them. This is a key point and what is called social confirmation.

So, on the off chance that you needed to impact your assistants or a specific group in your specialty or the new contracts, you have to get one of them to purchase in first. At the point when they see a worker such as themselves making a move without anyone else or following another mandate, they are increasingly plausible to go with the same pattern.

Having that first individual make a move has a significant effect and opens the intensity of social confirmation.

Authority

At the point when you are seen as a specialist in a region, others will be bound to concede to you. You may ask why? Frequently it is a belief that specialists can offer an alternate route to great choices that would somehow or another set aside a long effort to devise themselves. The thought at that point is to set up the validity of power and ability. Many people regularly botch this chance since they expect others will distinguish their ability consequently. You can't surrender it over to translation since it will frequently be neglected.

There are various approaches to build up such power. A speedy and simple one is to make unmistakable all recognitions, certifications, and grants in the workplace or work environment to set up your experience. This may not generally be an alternative. Another methodology is to pass on mastery through short accounts or foundation data partook in easygoing discussions. Simply recollect, your aptitude isn't constantly a known amount, so make certain to pass on it when you find the opportunity.

Scarcity

Individuals give higher esteem of what is rare. It's simply a fundamental organic market. As things become all the rarer, they getting increasingly important to other people. There are a couple of ways that you can utilize the standard of shortage to convince others. One is just to make offers restricted time, constrained supply, or one-time, which promptly makes a feeling of shortage.

Simultaneously, how you present such open doors matters as well. If you center more around misfortune language, or language that shows what you will miss out on as opposed to picking up, your message turns out to be all the more dominant. Lastly is the eliteness approach. Giving access to data, administrations, or different things to a constrained arrangement of individuals makes a feeling of eliteness. This regularly gets converted into being some help to those individuals or that you hold them in high esteem more than others.

If you can join these to outline a circumstance, your forces of influence significantly increase. So, attempt to use restricted offers, misfortune language, and selectiveness, to make a feeling of shortage.

Chapter 5: The Art of Using Your Mind to Succeed

The use of your mind is a profound discussion. Remember chapter two where we discussed NLP. You got that, you need to be fully aware of yourself and how your mind operates. Therefore, it will be easy to read other people's minds, manipulate them into positively taking action. In this way, you are also going to benefit. In this chapter, we look at how you can attract positive people in your life as well as make a positive impact. It is said that success is in your mind. You have to think and view yourself as a success.

Attracting Positive People in Your Life

To succeed in personal life and career, you must create a foundation of good vibes. It is not possible to have all-round success while you are a negative minded person. In this section, let us start by looking at the ways that you can attract positive people in your life.

Visualize Them

You'll as of now be comfortable with the way toward utilizing imaginative representation to manufacture point by point, exact pictures of the things you need to pull in. In any case, when you've sharpened your representation abilities, you can likewise utilize them to do different activities.

One method that can assist you with attracting positive minded individuals includes picturing these individuals coming towards you. After you've concentrated on moderate, relentless relaxing for a few moments, enable your psyche to create a picture that speaks to your capacity to pull other constructive individuals to you.

For instance, you may feel a sparkling feature of a vague individual holding their arms out in your direction. You may feel the affection and bolster that resounds from this individual. Then again, you may envision yourself gleaming with a brilliant light that attractively pulls in great individuals.

There's no standard about what you have to envision, as long as you feel it speaks to cheerful, supporting people coming into your life. Attempt to rehash this representation at any rate once every day.

Focus on Your Negativity

As the Law of Attraction states, we will in general draw in a greater amount of the things we "offer out" to the universe. In this way, if you're conveying a negative attitude, then it will be very hard for you to attract people that have a positive attitude. Also, remember that you will also attract negative things and this will hinder your personal development as well as in career. Therefore, if you notice that you are exuding a negative attitude, try and counter-attack it to ooze out positive energy. It will also make you attractive. Ask yourself whether you have any negative convictions or suppositions about fellowships and connections. At that point work to counter those to draw increasingly constructive individuals on your side.

Be Straightforward

At times, we clutch old kinships and connections that are never again working for our benefit but just pull us down. To have a high chance of meeting and interacting with positive people while making strong associations, practice a consistent regime of self-reflection about your group of friends. Is it accurate to say that anyone is hauling you down? Is there somebody who consistently censures you, or even snickers at you? It's a great opportunity to consider cutting ties with these sorts of individuals to make space for the individuals who will enable you and help you to arrive at your maximum capacity.

Allow Love Every Day

You can draw in increasingly constructive individuals towards you in case you're continually emanating energy even to outsiders. Make a routine for exuding love each day, and you'll see it start to return to you. You don't need to make stupendous signals even simply complimenting somebody on their lovely outfit, listening carefully to a friend in trouble for a few minutes or giving an hour of your free time to charitable effort every week can have a major effect. As a little something extra, these sorts of exercises may trigger great new fellowships!

Practice Affirmations Before Socializing

At last, you can get yourself into the correct headspace for making positive associations by giving yourself somewhat of a get-up and go talk before you mingle. Regardless of whether you're going to investing energy becoming acquainted with individuals at work, heading off to a gathering or going to supper, attempt to discover certifications that make you feel open and cheerful about the plausibility of becoming acquainted with individuals.

Concentrate on your best characteristics and the things that you realize other individuals acknowledge about you. Reaffirm your faith in these parts of yourself. For instance, you may state "I feel and trust the constructive vitality inside me" or "I can draw in positive individuals who will improve my life."

Skills in Leadership That Will Help You Influence People

After learning the art of attracting positive individuals in your life, you must get equipped with leadership skills that will strategically enhance your success in your career. Now, let us go through some of the tips that will help you enhance your leadership skills.

Leadership abilities can assume a huge role in the development of your career. Specialized aptitudes may just take you up until this point. To assist you with pushing ahead in your profession, you'll most likely need delicate aptitudes, for example, the capacity to be a decent pioneer. In this way, authority abilities are viewed as significant qualities that can assist you in getting to the highest point of your professional field. You're bound to be enlisted or get an advancement on the off chance that you've been effective in positions of authority in your expert or individual life.

Very few individuals are born as leaders. The greater part of us has to work on being a decent and successful leader, and that is the reason administration advancement is so significant. There is a wide range of sorts of leadership, and there are numerous ranges of abilities that can assist you with turning into an effective leader.

Stepping Up to the Task

Most managers will just allot workers the assignments they realize they can do. That is the reason it's advisable to volunteer to take on more obligations while going well beyond your present position. Concentrate on learning skills that fall outside your essential area of specialization. Keep in mind, the more you work, the more you learn new things. Finding out more and assuming greater liability will inevitably help move you into a position of authority in your working environment.

Become a Critical Thinker

To be contracted for a prominent activity, you should be a basic thinker. Great pioneers can anticipate the issue of potential even before they occur. They can likewise create approaches to keep issues from occurring. Great pioneers are likewise mindful of potential openings and exploit them to profit the organization and representatives.

Listening Effectively

One of the most significant abilities of a pioneer is being a good listener. Without listening abilities, you are not ready to get input from others and get a feeling of what colleagues like about the tasks they take a shot at.

Input is vital. To listen successfully, you have to keep in touch, maintain a strategic distance from interruptions and react fittingly. Remember, correspondence isn't just about verbal correspondence. Know about non-verbal communication and motions to figure out what individuals are truly saying.

Be an Inspiration

It is said that if your activities motivate others to dream more, find out additional, accomplish more and become more, you are indeed a leader.

A genuine leader ought to emphatically impact individuals. At the point when workers or collaborators lose their desire and interests, a genuine leader can motivate and persuade them. How do pioneers inspire individuals? To start with, they comprehend what individuals want and need. For instance, if a worker loses inspiration since the individual in question thinks their diligent work isn't being perceived, a great head will converse with that individual and offer the acknowledgment that is merited.

In some cases, individuals lose their inspiration since they are going through challenges, are worn out on doing the same redundant errands, or are frustrated they are not being approached to get included. As a pioneer, you should have a conversation with the staff member, and ask the person in question on what the matter is...and urge them to discover better approaches to get included.

Having the Discipline

Good discipline is required to execute the objective. Regardless of whether you have a dream or a smart thought, it's pointless without discipline. On the off chance that you need to have adequate execution as a leader, then you need discipline.

For instance, say you and your group needed to make a marketable strategy to draw in speculators. You had bunches of thoughts for the field-tested strategy, however, there was no control set up to guarantee the introduction was practiced. At the point when it came time to show the presentation, you were not ready to appropriately communicate your target to the willing investors. This result brought about the financial specialists declining your proposition. To be a decent pioneer, you should act in a well-disciplined manner, and ensure others in your group are taught. This will enhance your rating and propel you higher.

Consistent Learning

Leadership and learning are vital to one another. At the point when things are evolving quickly, it is critical to continually learn and challenge yourself. You have heard that, when you stop learning, you start dying. It is important to keep adding knowledge in your area of expertise.

Expertise to Delegate

The best top leader is the person who has the wisdom to select great men to do what he needs to be done and patience to keep from intruding with them as they perform the task.

Effective leaders will not micromanage. Representative work to your workers and lets them feel engaged. If you do this, they will feel progressively included and have a greater chance to grow new aptitudes. Designating will enable you to focus on the objectives you have to accomplish yourself. If you are an undertaking chief, you are as yet liable for the work at last. This is the reason it is essential to manage the task when assigning.

Dealing with Conflicts

As a leader, you need to realize how to deal with troublesome individuals and resolve battles. If a representative doesn't work to the best of their capacity and carries a negative attitude to the workplace, pioneers need to step up and converse with that individual in seclusion.

Leaders must be straightforward and direct. This requires a great deal of fearlessness. It is difficult to bring up an issue or lay off somebody, so make sure to consistently listen in to the staff's side of the story before you arrive at a resolution and make the next move.

Be a Follower

Leaders ought to figure out how to perceive the real value of colleagues, gain from them, and urge other colleagues to also learn and gain from them. Get the knowledge of the things that you did not know from an individual who has some expertise here.

Influencing All Kinds of People

It is hope for all of us that we can reach a point where we can influence people even when we do not have the authority in the place. Let us discuss what to do to get at this point.

In a universe of unpredictable, rambling associations, the sense of authority is not the same anymore. Without a doubt, you might be the head of the organization, however, you're having the title isn't sufficient to get individuals to do what you inquire. Furthermore, your direction is additionally weakened when you get to work in a group, team up across all the boundaries or depend on numerous partners. That is the reason individual impact is a basic ability in leadership.

The impact is the power and capacity to influence others' activities, choices, conclusions or thinking. At one level, it is about consistency, about getting somebody to oblige what you need them to do. Be that as it may, you regularly need real duty from others to achieve key objectives and errands.

Genuine responsibility implies you have had success with regards to influencing individuals so they'll underwrite and bolster you or your undertaking. Also, in the present violent economy, when you are frequently executing enormous change, curtailing assets, or managing intense difficulties, you need all the responsibility or commitment, you can get.

At the point when you impact individuals so they arrive at a position of taking real responsibility, working connections start to improve. You see more prominent supported exertion and versatility. Your associates become increasingly proficient, imaginative, and centered. How might you impact others, and move them from resisting to consistency to responsibility?

There have been three types of techniques that influence: That includes logical, emotional, and cooperative. This influence through the face, heart, and hands

Logical

A logical appeal draws on the purpose and wisdom of people. You put forward an argument centered on institutional advantages, financial benefits or even for the best option of action. Many of us understand how to vent our thoughts or plans' organizational benefits. With truthful and comprehensive proof for their practicability and significance, we discuss the reasons for our suggested actions rationally and logically. They clarify why these acts are the absolute best, simply and objectively. If questioned, they clarify how it is possible to address future organizational issues or concerns.

The specific logical attraction, outlining how the desired action can benefit an individual's long-term career, is less routine, but still common. You may go it a step further by helping the employee gain more exposure and a better image within the company or by making a job easier or interesting.
An emotional plea unites your statement, main objective, or task to values and goals that are individual. Guide your proposal to some other individual's straightforward and attractive vision. Define the task enthusiastically and convey faith in the ability of the individual to fulfill it.

To make a logical argument, of course, you should have some connection and comprehension with the individual you're talking to. An emotional appeal that is misguided or uninformed may backfire. Generally speaking, a concept that encourages the feeling of well-being, service or belonging of a person does have the finest chance to gain assistance.

A collaborative request creates a bond to get help for your idea between you, the individual you want to impact and many others. Continuing to work with each other to achieve a goal of mutual importance means that in the organization you are extending a hand to others. It's a very powerful way to influence. Developing cooperative relationships can involve collaborative work which includes figuring what you're going to do together, consulting which includes finding out what other people's views have and partnerships that are drawing on who already supports you or has the credibility you need.

All three approaches are known to be used by the most effective influencers: That is emotion, logic, and cooperation. You will also want to determine your type of control to increase your influence. Which tactics are you most using? What else could you do? When you rely solely on persuasive arguments, for instance, you might miss a chance to engage with people through their feelings, beliefs, and interactions. When you overemphasize emotional or collaborative arguments, you may be unaware of the evidence and justifications that make up your position.

Influencing at the Workplace

To advance your career, you need to know how to be of influence in the workplace. There are many kinds of people at a work set up, therefore being able to influence a large part of them is critical to your success.

Having influence is control. Regardless of what your identity is, the place you work, or what your expert objectives are, accomplishing more impact in the work environment is basic for progress. Being of impact in a group can assist you with cooperating all the more adequately. Having an impact in a supervisory position can make you increasingly regarded and acknowledged. Being of influence in a gathering can make your voice bound to be heard and recognized.

Influence has incalculable favorable circumstances, however picking up that impact, such as learning some skills, requires significant investment and exertion. Luckily, there are numerous procedures you can use to develop this characteristic.

1. Work to Develop Trust with Your Co-Workers

Being of influence is regularly and most effectively brought through trust. Just when an associate believes you will the person be available to your impact. In case you're in a higher place in your profession in the organization chain of command, it's, therefore, possible to pass on an interest or appoint an assignment that must be completed by your worker, yet obvious impact proposes a through and through freedom part.

If you appointed a similar undertaking yet didn't convey a more significant position of authority, would your representative still hear you out and accept that the assignment is important to undertake? This theory may not be important to your circumstance, however paying little heed to your situation in contrast with the places of your colleagues, if you need a sound and compelling working relationship, you will need to develop trust. The most effortless approach to do that will be transparency and being a person of integrity. Express your suppositions, unveil your misgivings, and don't keep any hidden information. It is very straightforward.

2. Through Consistency Develop Reliability

Irregularity is the quickest method to destroy your good reputation. Consistency, then again, is moderate and a sure way of doing things. If you execute your work adequately and on schedule, for a long time, in the end, individuals will come to depend on you. The equivalent is genuine when you execute a predictable style of authority, setting reliable desires with your representatives and giving steady rewards for good work. Individuals will come to depend on your conduct and anticipate that you should be a predictable entertainer.

The act of consistency is crucial for building impact. If not, you'll have a history of not predictable, and individuals won't realize whether to trust or decline your recommendations. In case you're reliably roused by similar standards, individuals will believe that your thoughts are strong and dependable as an expansion, and that will make it simpler to get individuals on your side. Consistency is particularly significant when you are in a much less position since it exhibits a level of commitment.

3. Aim to be Assertive and Not Aggressive

Being assertive is the best way to get your thoughts noticeable, particularly when you're contending with others for being visible, for example, in a meeting. There is a contrast between being assertive and being aggressive. You'll have to exhibit your considerations and thoughts with a high level of certainty, demonstrating your feelings, yet any over the top level of certainty could be confused with unnecessary self-importance, which will be a compromise to your apparent power. Track cautiously, particularly when you're new to your group of spectators or in case you're displaying your musings on a zone outside of your ability.

This confidence ought to stretch out as a general quality to every one of your interactions, paying little mind to whether you're addressing workers above, underneath, or at your level, and paying little mind to the discussion group. Being self-assured, since you have confidence in what you're stating, is an approach to develop the notoriety of power and gain the capacity to impact your companions and work colleagues.

4. You Should be Flexible

Adaptability is very significant. While this may appear as though it clashes with the urge to presenting assertiveness, it's hard to stand up for yourself completely in case you're available to changing your ideas and opinions being excessively stringent or determined in your convictions will neutralize you. For this situation, individuals will come to consider you to be a difficult, relentless stone monument, unequipped for trusting in anybody other than yourself. This can diminish the regard individuals have for you and bargain your general impact.

Rather, work effectively to show your adaptability while holding firm on your convictions. Arrangements and bargains are frequently the most ideal approaches to do this. Remain inflexible in your convictions when somebody repudiates you, yet work with them to discover a commonly satisfactory arrangement. At the point when individuals trust you to be adaptable, they'll be bound to hear you out regardless of whether they're obstinate in their very own right.

5. Strive to be Personal

A little character goes far, particularly when you're attempting to assemble impact in the working environment. This is particularly significant when you're in a higher situation, as a chief or a manager. If you confine yourself or attempt to construct your apparent authority by separating yourself from the others, it may just serve to estrange you and set you in a place where you're seen with doubt or even disdain.

Rather, make a special effort to have individual trades with your representatives and workers. You don't have to develop good relationships, however, there's no motivation as to why you can't become acquainted with one another. Individual working connections are significant for developing a feeling of group, and if individuals consider you to be someone else in the group, they'll be progressively open when you uncover your thoughts or assessments. The key here is to appear to be flawed, human and approachable.

6. Concentrate on Actions Rather Than Argument

Attempting to assemble impact through words is pointless. Indeed, even a leader with the most perfect expression and a foundation in explanatory procedure can't want to win the impact of their friends through discourses and contentions alone. In case you're going to assemble impact in the working environment, you have to talk through your actions, or at any rate have the action deeds and history to back up whatever it is you're stating.

Some portion of this becomes an integral factor when you develop consistency. Having a good work ethic that is consistent and productive and getting reliably great outcomes shows individuals that you're ready to walk the walk. Showing your thoughts through genuine models is the following stage in this procedure. Rather than contending about how your structure will function in principle, put it under serious scrutiny.

7. Be a Good Listener

At last, recall that impact is two-way. The more you trust in the individuals around you and consolidate their thoughts into your vision, the more they'll put stock in your thoughts and join them into their work propensities. If you need to develop this sort of association with your colleagues and representatives, you initially need to be listening. Tune in to everybody's conclusion, and urge individuals to make comments on what they think, particularly if they don't regularly voice their ideas. Set aside some effort to regard and recognize everyone's supposition, and let individuals realize that you hold them in high esteem.

This makes a climate of common trust, shared regard, and common collaboration. In case you're initiating the activity to construct this condition, they'll come to consider you to be a pioneer, and your sentiments will normally be heard, recognized, and regarded accordingly.

Having influence is an exceptional resource in the expert world, yet always remember, your objective here ought to be increasingly given respect in the work environment, not to improve the probability of having others do your pitching. One is a decent adventure to more prominent noticeable quality and productivity, while the other is a Machiavellian power trip.

Chapter 6: Manipulation theories

Amplification Theory

During my day to day work, I deal with a lot of people. I have noticed something while in forums or public discussions. I saw that when individuals state something frequently and with validity, others started to trust it. I pondered this and chose to do a little research. I inevitably went over something known as the amplification theory. Its possibility is that if you express a specific view with sureness and authority the view solidifies and spreads to other people. This thought relates especially well to the spread of political perspectives on majority rule stages, for example, the web. At the point when individuals express their perspectives with power, others are bound to concur with their perspectives.

The Conversion Theory

A moderately little gathering of suffragettes contended emphatically for the at first disagreeable view that ladies ought to be permitted to cast a ballot. The diligent work of the suffragettes, joined with the equity of their case, at last, drove the lion's share to acknowledge their perspective.

Similarity studies include a minority bunch who was adjusting to the dominant part. Moscovici contended along various lines. He guaranteed that Asch (1951) and others had put a lot of accentuation on the thought that the dominant party in a gathering impacts the minority. As he would see it, it is likewise workable for a minority to impact the larger part.

Truth be told Asch concurred with Moscovici. He also felt that minority impact did happen and that it was conceivably an increasingly important issue to examine to concentrate on why a few people may pursue minority feelings and oppose a gathering pressure.

Moscovici made a differentiation among compliance and conversion. Compliance is normal in congruity research for example Asch whereby the members freely comply with the gathering standards however secretly dismiss them.

The conversion includes how a minority can impact the dominant group. It includes persuading the majority part that the minority perspectives are right. This can be accomplished in various ways for example consistency, adaptability. Conversion is something different from consistence as it, for the most part, includes both open and private acknowledgment of another view or conduct.

How does the minority change the view of the majority?
Moscovici contends that a lion's share impact will, in general, be founded on open compliance. It is probably going to be an instance of standardizing social impact. In this regard, the intensity of numbers is significant, the side of the majority can compensate and accept with an endorsement as well as to object. What's more, in light of this there is pressure on minorities to adjust. Since the majority frequently do not care about the minorities' opinion of them, minority impact is seldom founded on regularizing social impact. Rather, it is normally founded on educational social impact giving the majority new thoughts, new data which leads them to rethink their perspectives. In this regard, minority impact includes private acknowledgment changing over the larger part by persuading them that the minority's perspectives are correct.
Four primary components have been distinguished as significant for a minority to have an impact on the majority.

These are social style, style of reasoning, adaptability, and recognizable proof.

The Behavioral Style
This involves 4 segments:

- Being consistent: The minority must be steady as they would like to think
- Trust in the rightness of thoughts and perspectives they are displaying
- Giving off an impression of being objective
- Opposing social weight and misuse

Moscovici further expressed that one of the most significant parts of the behavioral style is the consistency with which individuals hold their position. Being steady and constant in a view is bound to impact the dominant part than if a minority is conflicting and cleaves and alters their perspective.

Moscovici (1969) explored social styles (reliable/conflicting) on minority impact in his blue-green examinations. He demonstrated that a steady minority was more effective than a conflicting minority in changing the perspectives on the larger part.

Consistency might be significant because:

- Confronted with predictable resistance, individuals from the majority side will sit up, pay heed, and reevaluate their position.

- Consistency gives the feeling that the minority are persuaded they are correct and are focused on their perspective.

To change the greater part's view the minority needs to propose an unmistakable position and needs to safeguard and backer its position reliably.

A qualification can be made between two types of consistency:

- **The Diachronic Consistency** - This is consistency over some time. The larger part stocks to its firearms don't change its perspectives.

- **The Synchronic Consistency** - This is consistency between its individuals. In this, all individuals concur and back one another up.

Style of Thinking

Recognize three or four minority gatherings for example refuge searchers, British National Party and so forth. How would you think and react to every one of these minority gatherings and the perspectives they set forward? Do you expel their perspectives inside and out or consider what they need to state and talk about their perspectives with other individuals?

If you reject the perspectives on other individuals without really thinking about them, you would have occupied with shallow ideas/preparing. On the other hand, if you had considered the perspectives being advanced, you would have occupied with precise reasoning/preparing. Research has indicated that if a minority can get the larger part to consider an issue and consider contentions for and against, at that point the minority stands a decent possibility of affecting the dominant part. If the minority can get the majority to talk about and banter the contentions that the minority are advancing, the impact is probably going to be more grounded.

- Also, when the majority is stood up by somebody with self-assurance and commitment to take a prominent stand and will not back claim, they may expect that the individual in question has a point.

- Reliable minority upsets built up to standards and make the situation uncertain and strife. This can prompt the greater part paying attention to the minority see.

The majority will consequently be bound to scrutinize their perspectives.

Flexibility and Compromise

Various scientists have addressed whether consistency alone is adequate for a minority to impact a larger part. They contend that the key is the way the dominant part deciphers consistency. If the reliable minority is viewed as a firm, inflexible, solid, and opinionated, they will probably not change the perspectives on the dominant part. On the other hand, if they seem adaptable and trading off, they are probably going to be viewed as less outrageous, as increasingly moderate, agreeable, and sensible. Accordingly, they will have a superior possibility of changing the views of the majority. A few scientists have gone further and recommended that it isn't only the presence of flexibility and compromise which is significant but also flexibility and compromise.

This probability was examined by Nemeth in 1986. The analysis depended on a counterfeit jury wherein gatherings of three members and one confederate needed to settle on the measure of pay to be given to the casualty of a ski-lift mishap. At the point when the predictable minority contended for a low sum and would not change his position, he had no impact on the larger part. In any case, when he bargained and moved some route towards the greater part position, the lion's share additionally undermined and changed their view. This trial addresses the significance of consistency. The minority position transformed, it was not reliable, and it was this change brought about minority impact.

Identification

Individuals keep an eye on the character with individuals who seem like themselves. For instance, men will, in general, relate to men, girls with girls, youngsters with their fellow adolescents and so forth. Research demonstrates that if the dominant part relates to the minority, at that point they are bound to pay attention to the perspectives on the minority and change their very own perspectives following those of the minority.

For instance, one examination indicated that a gay minority contending for gay rights had less effect on a straight majority than a straight minority contending for gay rights. The majority who are non-gay related to the non-gay minority. They would, in general, consider the to be a minority as not quite the same as themselves, as self-intrigued and worried about advancing their specific reason.

Information Manipulation Theory

This theory entails one of several four communicative maxims being intentionally broken by a persuasive person.
These are all four:

- **Quantity:** This means that the information provided is accurate and full of data.
- **Quality:** Accurate and truthful information.
- **Relationship:** Communication knowledge is important.
- **Manner:** Information is publicly available and understood, also non-verbal acts help the declaration's tone

Priming

In the field of psychology and manipulation of the mind, priming is a strategy wherein the presentation of one upgrade impacts how individuals react to a resulting improvement. Preparing works by initiating an affiliation or portrayal in memory just before another improvement or errand is presented. This wonder happens without our cognizant mindfulness, yet it can majorly affect various parts of our regular day to day existence.

What is Priming?

There is a wide range of instances of how this priming function. For instance, presenting somebody with the "yellow" will summon a quicker reaction to thinking of a "banana" than it would to inconsequential words like "TV." Because yellow and banana are all the more firmly connected in memory, individuals react quicker when the subsequent word is introduced.

Preparing can work with boosts that are connected in an assortment of ways. For instance, priming impacts can happen with perceptually, in linguistics, or conceptually related improvements. Preparing can have promising genuine applications as a learning and study help too.

Priming is named a such to bring out the symbolism of priming water well. When the well has been prepared, water would then be able to be hence created at whatever point it is turned on. When data has been prepared in memory, it tends to be recovered into mindfulness all the more promptly.

Sorts of Priming

There are a few distinct sorts of priming in psychology and mind manipulation. Everyone works with a particular goal in mind and may have various impacts.

Positive and negative priming portray how priming impacts handling speed. Positive priming makes handling quicker and accelerates memory recovery, while negative priming backs it off.

Semantic priming includes words that are related to legitimately or etymologically. The prior case of reacting to "banana" all the more quickly in the wake of being prepared with "yellow" is a case of semantic priming.

Acquainted preparing includes utilizing two improvements that are regularly connected. For instance, cat and mouse are two words that are regularly connected in memory, so the presence of one of the words can take action to react all the more quickly when the subsequent word shows up.

Reiteration priming happens when an upgrade and reaction are more than once matched. Along these lines, subjects become bound to react with a particular goal in mind all the more rapidly each time the boost shows up.

Perceptual priming includes boosts that have comparable structures. For instance, "goat" will bring out a quicker reaction when it is gone before by "boat" because the two words are perceptually comparative.

Reasonable preparing includes a boost and reaction that are thoughtfully related. Words, for example, "work area" and "seat" are probably going to show preparing impacts since they are in the equivalent applied classification.

The masked priming includes some portion of the underlying upgrade being darkened somehow or another, for example, with hash marks. Even though the whole upgrade isn't obvious, regardless it brings out a reaction. Words in which certain letters are clouded are one case of priming that is masked.

The Priming Process

Therapists accept that units (or patterns) of data are put away in long haul memory. The actuation of these compositions can either be expanded or diminished in an assortment of ways. At the point when the initiation of specific units of data is expanded, these recollections become simpler to get to. At the point when actuation is diminished, the data turns out to be less inclined to be recovered from memory.

Priming states that specific patterns will, in general, be initiated as one. By actuating a few units of data, related or associated units likewise become dynamic. So, for what reason would it be helpful for related compositions to become initiated and progressively open? In numerous examples, having the option to bring related data into memory all the more rapidly may assist individuals with reacting quicker when the need emerges.

For instance, the schemas identified with rainstorms and smooth streets might be connected intently in memory. At the point when you see that it is coming down, recollections about conceivable smooth street conditions may ring a bell also. Since your psyche has been prepared to think about this data, you may be better ready to think rapidly and respond quickly when you experience a risky, wet stretch of street on your commute home from work.

Genuine Impact

Priming has been seen in an assortment of courses in brain research inquire about labs, however, what effect does it truly have in reality?

Preparing Can Influence How You Perceive the World

The viral marvel of Yanny and Laurel is one case of how preparing can impact how you see data. An equivocal sound example was transferred by an online client with a survey asking what individuals heard. A few people particularly heard "Yanny," while others heard "Tree." Some individuals even revealed having the option to switch to and from between which words they heard.

Because of the aural uncertainty, clinicians propose that individuals depend on priming impacts to help figure out what they are bound to hear. The research proposes that we don't hear by breaking down the frequencies of the commotions that enter our ears and afterward deciding the words that these frequencies structure. Rather, we use what is referred to as top-down handling. Our cerebrums initially perceive a few sounds as discourse. At that point, our minds use setting prompts to decipher the significance of these discourse sounds.

This can help clarify why individuals regularly confound melody verses. At the point when the sound is questionable, your cerebrum fills in the missing data admirably well. The priming impacts would then be able to become possibly the most important factor. If you are prepared to decipher a verse with a specific goal in mind, you will be bound to hear it with a particular goal in mind dependent on that priming.

With regards to hearing either Yanny or Laurel, simply monitoring the idea of the viral sound clasp primes you to hear it as either of the two. The way that individuals who heard the clip were at that point hoping to hear either Yanny or Laurel primed them to hear both of those two words and not some other word.

For this situation, factors identified with sound quality and hearing capacity additionally assumed a role. More youthful individuals with less age-related hearing harm were bound to hear "Yanny" because their ears are better ready to distinguish higher recurrence sounds. The individuals who heard Laurel kept an eye on just hear lower-recurrence sounds.

Priming Can Have an Influence in Your Behavior in Various Ways

In one examination, scientists verifiably prepared members with words generally connected with generalizations about older individuals. After leaving the testing stall, individuals who had been primed with words identified with more seasoned grown-ups were bound to walk more gradually than members who had not been prepared.

One study distributed in the diary Aging and Mental Health found that preparing members with negative maturing generalizations brought about progressively negative impacts on practices and self-appraised assessments. Preparing members with these negative maturing generalizations prompted expanded sentiments of forlornness and an expanded recurrence in help-chasing.

Inferring generalizations about old individuals being in a situation of loneliness, and powerless, prompted individuals feeling lonelier and acting increasingly vulnerable. Scientists propose that being presented to such age-related generalizations may prompt expanded reliance and lower self-assessments of capacity and work in more established individuals.

Priming is Also Useful as a Tool for Education

Instructors and academicians can likewise use priming as a learning apparatus. A few students perform better when they recognize what they can anticipate. Handling new material can now and then scare, however preparing understudies by displaying data before an exercise is given can help.

Priming is regularly utilized as an instructive mediation for the students with certain learning inabilities. New material is introduced before it is instructed, enabling the understudy to become OK with it. For instance, the learners may be permitted to "review" the books or materials that will be utilized as a component of an exercise. Since they are now acquainted with the data and materials, they might be better ready to focus during the genuine exercise.

Reciprocity Norm

The standard of reciprocity here and there alluded to as the standard of reciprocity, is a social standard where if somebody accomplishes something for you, you at that point feel committed to give back in kind. One territory where this standard is usually utilized is in the practice of marketing.

Advertisers use a wide scope of systems to persuade buyers to make buys. Some are clear, for example, deals, coupons, and uncommon advancements. Others are unmistakably progressively unpretentious and utilize standards of the human brain science of which numerous individuals are not by any means mindful.

This is how it works. Have you at any point felt committed to accomplishing something for somebody since they previously accomplished something for you? The standard of correspondence is only one kind of social standard that can impact our conduct. Reciprocity standard works on a straightforward rule: We will, in general, feel committed to returning support after individuals do favors for us. At the point when your new neighbors bring over a plate of treats to invite you to the area, you may feel committed to give back in kind.

Instances of Reciprocity in Real Life
- A salesman giving a complimentary gift to a potential client, trusting that it will lead them to give back in kind by buying something
- A pioneer offering consideration and mentorship to supporters in return for reliability
- Offering clients some important data in return for pursuing future marketing offers

Such conduct has a couple of clear benefits. For a certain something, dealing with others helps the endurance of the species. By responding, we guarantee that other individuals get help when they need it and that we get help when we require it. Reciprocity additionally enables individuals to complete things that they would not have the option to do alone. By cooperating or trading administrations, individuals can achieve more than they would exclusively.

Importance of Helping Others

Persuasion and Reciprocity

Various influence methods utilize the strategy of correspondence. These methodologies are utilized by individuals who are attempting to convince you to make a move or adjust with a solicitation, for example, sales reps or government officials.

One of these is known as the 'that is not all' system. Suppose you're looking for another cell phone. The sales rep shows your telephone and discloses to you the cost, yet you're as yet not exactly sure. On the off chance that the sales rep offers to include a telephone case at no extra charge, you may feel like he's helping you out, which thusly may make you feel committed to purchasing the telephone.

Would You be Able to Resist Reciprocity?

Much of the time, the reciprocity standard is something to be thankful for. It encourages us to carry on in a socially satisfactory manner and enables us to participate in a social give-and-take with the individuals around us. Be that as it may, what would it be advisable for you to do if you are attempting to beat the desire to respond, for example, attempting to maintain a strategic distance from the need to buy a thing in the wake of accepting a complimentary gift?

A few hints that can help:
Take some more time. Specialists propose that the desire to respond is most grounded following the underlying trade. If you can pause, you will likely feel less strain to give back in kind.
Assess the trade. Consider whether the support measures up to the normal return. As a rule, the underlying blessing or support is a lot littler than the mentioned return support.
At last, know that taking part in that first complementary trade can make it almost certain that you'll react to other, frequently greater, demands later on. In advertising, this is frequently called the "Foot in the Door" strategy. Somebody starts by

making a little solicitation, and once you consent to it, they at that point make a lot greater solicitation.

Scarcity Principle

Scarcity implies that things are progressively alluring when their accessibility is restricted. Scarcity is a word we know from financial matters.

None of us can have all that we need when we need it. We experience a daily reality such that shortage is our world. It doesn't make a difference how brilliant you are, what school you went to, or how composed you are. Regardless you face a shortage. The entirety of your decisions brings expenses and tradeoffs. Nothing is free.

While this is valid, we regularly don't feel the impacts of the shortage. If our nearby store doesn't have the item we need, the following one most likely will or we could arrange it on the web. If the café at which we are eating is out of the particular dinner we requested, they still most likely have a lot of nourishment so we could arrange our subsequent option feast.

Along these lines, scarcity is regularly falsely made. You've gotten those messages. There is a 50 percent off everything until late! Get one free while supplies last! The first 50 purchases have a gift.

This counterfeit shortage will in general urge individuals to settle on choices instead of keeping pondering them. I could consider which vehicle I need to purchase for quite a long time, however on the off chance that there is an exceptional deal going on, I'll presumably hustle just a bit and settle on a decision to benefit from the reserve funds.

This exposes another significant feature of influence that is valid in these standards, yet is especially pertinent here. Influence isn't controlled. The last degrades human respect.

As another financial analyst companion of our own, Dr. Craftsmanship Carden, says, the exchange is made of win. Influence similarly, encourages win-win circumstances. In case I'm in the market to purchase a vehicle, the fake shortage of a deal may convince me to settle on a choice sooner than I would have something else, however, I win by getting a vehicle and setting aside cash and the vehicle vendor wins by selling me a vehicle.

In case I'm in the market needing to purchase an item, as in the model from the primary blog in this arrangement, the experience that is made when the salespersons offer me a free example of their item may have convinced me to purchase their image, however it didn't constrain me without wanting to purchase that item.

A large number of these models originate from the universe of promoting, yet these standards of influence can completely be applied in an assortment of situations in which you may get yourself. Consider them when you are blogging, giving an introduction, or meeting for an occupation.

The Sleeper Effects

The sleeper impact is a term that alludes to the impact that a snippet of data that you at first disposed of as false has on you. As indicated by certain theories, this impact includes somebody at first overlooking a message that doesn't appear to be dependable. On the other hand, they in the long run come to accept the data they accepted to be false. This change can come to fruition because of new outer proof that supports the case. Then again, it can emerge out of interior thoughts that push you to rethink the data.

This system can appear to be somewhat conflicting because you will in general question messages that you at first don't accept more than those you do. In any case, this doesn't imply that a few snippets of data that are put away in your memory won't some time or another be significant, regardless of whether you at first trusted them to be questionable. They begin to become noteworthy when you find other information that makes you alter your perspective.

Some solid research shows that the convincing impact of a message is at its most elevated just after you get the message.

Likewise, you would expect that the additional time passes, the more the impact diminishes. Promoters know this. That is the reason they frequently offer some rewards to the individuals who buy rapidly.

Two Basic Conditions are Required for this Principle to Work

A solid starting effect: the sleeper impact possibly rises if the enticing message has a solid introductory effect. This is because a solid impression ensures it'll remain in memory and more time.

A message we see as the presence of mind: when the wellspring of the data isn't dependable, you will in general ruin the message. By and by, if you find that the source isn't trustworthy simply in the wake of having seen the motion picture, at that point, you'll be increasingly responsive to the messages and furthermore progressively suggestible.

Promoters know this reality well indeed. For instance, they can post an article on the advantages of chocolate to persuade individuals to eat a greater amount of it. Toward the finish of the article, they uncover that the essayist's associated with an organization that makes chocolate. So, when you get an enticing message before knowing its source, you'll be increasingly subject to encounter the sleeper impact.

The clarification for this marvel may be basic. Some state that your brain, over the long haul, overlooks that the wellspring of the data wasn't reliable. All things considered, the data itself remains. This is the motivation behind why you become increasingly powerless to accepting information from untrustworthy sources later on instead of when you originally read it.

The sleeper impact is one of the manners by which ads and the media can convince you to focus on something. It can likewise make you purchase things or decisions in favor of a particular applicant. Moreover, this marvel can cause you to disregard the terrible pieces of the item they're advertising.

Social Influence

Analysts have gone through decades concentrating the intensity of social impact, and how it controls individuals' conclusions and conduct. In particular, social influence alludes to how people change their thoughts and activities to satisfy the needs of a social gathering, saw authority, social job or a minority inside a gathering using impact over the dominant part.

The majority of us experience social impact in its numerous structures all the time. For instance, a learner may modify their conduct to coordinate that of different students in a class. The lion's share held assessments of a gathering of companions are probably going to advise the perspectives regarding new individuals to that social gathering. Moreover, we are affected by the solicitations of individual who are viewed as holding places of power. For example, a representative will pursue the sets of his bosses to satisfy them.

Why Individuals Acknowledge the Social Impact

There are various reasons why individuals enable social impacts to influence their contemplations and conduct.

One reason is that we regularly fit in with the standards of a gathering to pick up the acknowledgment of its individuals. Supporters of a football crew intentionally wear shirts of their groups to feel a piece of the gathering. Companions may likewise wear a comparative dress to their friends to encounter a feeling of having a place and accentuate their common thoughts.

Gathering similarity can likewise urge collaboration when endeavoring to accomplish a mutual objective. At the point when an individual can show a minority impact over a more extensive gathering, the person in question can convince that gathering to work all in all. For instance, philanthropy coordinators enrolling new volunteers promoters improving their locale (for example litter picking) in a way that can't be accomplished as effectively by only one individual acting alone.

Be that as it may, collaboration can prompt a similarity of perspectives, bringing about a wonder known as oblivious conformity. At the point when this happens, colleagues receive concurred perspectives and activities in the quest for a given objective, however, dismiss analysis from people who contradict or question the gathering's conduct. This absence of basic reasoning can negatively affect a gathering's presentation as its capacity to assess its very own conduct and adjust to changing conditions is blocked.

Furthermore, bunch similarity empowers a feeling of a union inside the general public. Laws disallowing brutality and burglary help to ensure each person inside a network. Notwithstanding, such laws rely upon individuals complying with the standards of the more extensive gathering by going about as well as behaved residents.
While social impact can positively affect conduct, its burdens have been a spurring factor behind the investigation into congruity by analysts, for example, Stanley Milgram.

Adjustment to a thin arrangement of practices and perspectives can demoralize the sustaining of new thoughts which could improve the lives of a gathering. It can demoralize its individuals from addressing and discussing the convictions and held by most of a gathering and its practices. This conduct has been seen in religions, where individuals are regularly hesitant to question the gathering's position publicly because of a paranoid fear of being dismissed by their companions.

Conclusion

You have made it to the end of Dark Psychology. This is a book that will help you in discovering yourself and further having the knowledge of manipulating people. Thank you for reading it to the end, let's hope it was informative and able to provide you with all of the tools you need to achieve your goals whatever they may be.

The next step is to take action and start practicing what you have read. Remember that charity begins at home. You do not want to receive all the goodness from the people while you cannot give them any value. Chapter one discusses the gist of dark psychology. You have learned about persuasion and what you should do to persuade people to take action. It is therefore important to fill your cup. Get the knowledge of your area of expertise. This will be done by becoming aware of you. This is more on NLP which is discussed in chapter two. Here you have been able to learn your mind and the reactions that you have in different circumstances. Further, you have got the knowledge of the connection between NLP and manipulation.

In chapter three, you have learned about the psychology of manipulation. Sometimes, people are to manipulate you negatively. Be it in a love relationship or at work. How do you take note of these manipulators and take control by guarding yourself? This was answered in this chapter. In line with this, chapter four discussed mind controls. These are the techniques that manipulators use to control your mind. You have learned of brainwashing, hypnosis, persuasion and much more.

In chapter five, you have learned on the art of seduction to be of influence on people and cause them to take action. This, in turn, propels your life and career. Finally, chapter six discusses the theories of manipulation. Here you have learned more about what happens in our daily life and what that means as a principle.

Finally, if you found this book useful in any way, a review on Amazon is always appreciated!

Thank you!